THE TURN OF
THE SCREW
&
DAISY MILLER

Henry James

SPARKNOTES is a registered trademark of SparkNotes LLC

Spark Educational Publishing
A Division of Barnes & Noble Publishing
120 Fifth Avenue
New York, NY 10011

ISBN 1-4114-0252-9

Please submit all comments and questions or report errors to *www.sparknotes.com/errors*

Printed and bound in the United States

CONTENTS

THE TURN OF THE SCREW

DAISY MILLER

THE TURN OF THE SCREW

CONTEXT

Henry James (1843–1916), whose mastery of the psychological novel markedly influenced twentieth-century literature, was born in New York City. His father, Henry James, Sr., was an unconventional thinker who had inherited considerable wealth. James, Sr., became a follower of Swedenborgian mysticism, a belief system devoted to the study of philosophy, theology, and spiritualism, and socialized with such eminent writers as Thomas Carlyle, Ralph Waldo Emerson, Henry David Thoreau, Washington Irving, and William Makepeace Thackeray. James's older brother, William James, profoundly influenced the emerging science of psychology through his *Principles of Psychology* (1890) and *The Varieties of Religious Experience* (1902). He also distinguished himself as an exponent of a brand of philosophical pragmatism he named "radical empiricism," the idea that beliefs do not work because they are true but are true because they work.

The James children were educated in a variety of schools and with private tutors, in what James later called "small vague spasms" of schooling augmented by his father's extensive library. In 1855 the James family began a three-year tour of Geneva, London, and Paris, an experience that probably influenced James's later preference for Europe over his native land. After a year at Harvard Law School, he began writing short stories and book reviews. He continued to travel widely from a base in England, where he chose to settle. He became a British subject in 1915, a year before his death at the age of seventy-three. By the time James died, he had written more than a hundred short stories and novellas, as well as literary and dramatic criticism, plays, travel essays, book reviews, and twenty novels, including *The Portrait of a Lady* (1881), *The Bostonians* (1886), *The Wings of the Dove* (1902), *The Ambassadors* (1903), and *The Golden Bowl* (1904).

Although James had many friends and acquaintances, he maintained a certain reserve toward most people. An "obscure hurt," as James later described a mysterious early injury he suffered in connection with a stable fire, haunted him throughout his life. He never married, and the absence of any known romantic attachments has led some critics to speculate that he was a repressed or closeted homosexual. Others attribute the reason for James's lifelong celibacy to the early death of his beloved cousin Mary "Minny" Temple, the model for several of his heroines.

James wrote *The Turn of the Screw* in 1897, at a low point in his life. In 1895 he had suffered a tremendous personal and professional blow when his play *Guy Domville* was booed off the London stage. Deeply wounded, James retreated from London and took refuge in Sussex, eventually taking a long-term lease on a rambling mansion called Lamb House. Shortly thereafter, he began writing *The Turn of the Screw*, one of several works from this period that revolve around large, rambling houses.

Like many writers and intellectuals of the time, James was fascinated by "spiritual phenomena," a field that was taken very seriously and was the subject of much "scientific" inquiry. The field remained popular even after the unmasking of the Fox sisters, whose claims of being able to communicate with the spirit world had started the craze for spiritualism in the 1840s. Henry James, Sr., and William James were both members of the Society for Psychical Research, and William served as its president from 1894 to 1896.

James had written ghost stories before *The Turn of the Screw*. It was a popular form, especially in England, where, as the prologue to *The Turn of the Screw* suggests, gathering for the purpose of telling ghost stories was something of a Christmastide tradition. According to James's notebooks and his preface to the 1908 edition of *The Turn of the Screw*, the germ of the story had been a half-remembered anecdote told to him by Edward White Benson, the archbishop of Canterbury: a story of small children haunted by the ghosts of a pair of servants who wish them ill.

In Benson's story, the evil spirits repeatedly tried to lure the children to their deaths. The spin James put on the story was to make everything—the presence of the ghosts, their moral depravity, their designs on the children—purely a function of hearsay. As careful readers have noted, the ghosts are visible only to one person in the tale—the governess who serves as both narrator and protagonist.

The Turn of the Screw first appeared in *Collier's Weekly* in twelve installments between January and April 1898. Not until after World War I did anyone question the reliability of the governess as a narrator. With the publication of a 1934 essay by the influential critic Edmund Wilson, a revised view of the story began to gain currency. Wilson's Freudian interpretation, that the governess is a sexually repressed hysteric and the ghosts mere figments of her overly excitable imagination, echoed what other critics like Henry Beers, Harold Goddard, and Edna Kenton had previously suggested in the 1920s. Throughout the course of his life, Wilson continued to revise and rethink his interpretation of *The Turn of the Screw*, but all criticism since has had to confront the central ambiguity in the narrative. Is the governess a hopeless neurotic who hallucinates the figures of Peter Quint and Miss Jessel, or is she a plucky young woman battling to save her charges from damnation? Adherents of both views abound, though the former take on the story is rarer. Other critics maintain that the beauty and terror of the tale reside in its utter ambiguity, arguing that both interpretations are possible and indeed necessary to make *The Turn of the Screw* the tour de force that it is.

PLOT OVERVIEW

An anonymous narrator recalls a Christmas Eve gathering at an old house, where guests listen to one another's ghost stories. A guest named Douglas introduces a story that involves two children—Flora and Miles—and his sister's governess, with whom he was in love. After procuring the governess's written record of events from his home, he provides a few introductory details. A handsome bachelor persuaded the governess to take a position as governess for his niece and nephew in an isolated country home after the previous governess died. Douglas begins to read from the written record, and the story shifts to the governess's point of view as she narrates her strange experience.

The governess begins her story with her first day at Bly, the country home, where she meets Flora and a maid named Mrs. Grose. The governess is nervous but feels relieved by Flora's beauty and charm. The next day she receives a letter from her employer, which contains a letter from Miles's headmaster saying that Miles cannot return to school. The letter does not specify what Miles has done to deserve expulsion, and, alarmed, the governess questions Mrs. Grose about it. Mrs. Grose admits that Miles has on occasion been bad, but only in the ways boys ought to be. The governess is reassured as she drives to meet Miles.

One evening, as the governess strolls around the grounds, she sees a strange man in a tower of the house and exchanges an intense stare with him. She says nothing to Mrs. Grose. Later, she catches the same man glaring into the dining-room window, and she rushes outside to investigate. The man is gone, and the governess looks into the window from outside. Her image in the window frightens Mrs. Grose, who has just walked into the room. The governess discusses her two experiences with Mrs. Grose, who identifies the strange man as Peter Quint, a former valet who is now dead.

Convinced that the ghost seeks Miles, the governess becomes rigid in her supervision of the children. One day, when the governess is at the lake with Flora, she sees a woman dressed in black and senses that the woman is Miss Jessel, her dead predecessor. The governess is certain Flora was aware of the ghost's presence but intentionally kept quiet. The governess again questions Mrs. Grose about

Miles's misbehavior. Mrs. Grose reveals that Quint had been "too free" with Miles, and Miss Jessel with Flora. The governess is on her guard, but the days pass without incident, and Miles and Flora express increased affection for the governess.

The lull is broken one evening when something startles the governess from her reading. She rises to investigate, moving to the landing above the staircase. There, a gust of wind extinguishes her candle, and she sees Quint halfway up the stairs. She refuses to back down, exchanging another intense stare with Quint until he vanishes. Back in her room, the governess finds Flora's bed curtains pulled forward, but Flora herself is missing. Noticing movement under the window blind, the governess watches as Flora emerges from behind it. The governess questions Flora about what she's been doing, but Flora's explanation is unrevealing.

The governess does not sleep well during the next few nights. One night, she sees the ghost of Miss Jessel sitting on the bottom stair, her head in her hands. Later, when the governess finally allows herself to go to sleep at her regular hour, she is awoken after midnight to find her candle extinguished and Flora by the window. Careful not to disturb Flora, the governess leaves the room to find a window downstairs that overlooks the same view. Looking out, she sees the faraway figure of Miles on the lawn.

Later, the governess discusses with Mrs. Grose her conversation with Miles, who claimed that he wanted to show the governess that he could be "bad." The governess concludes that Flora and Miles frequently meet with Miss Jessel and Quint. At this, Mrs. Grose urges the governess to appeal to her employer, but the governess refuses, reminding her colleague that the children's uncle does not want to be bothered. She threatens to leave if Mrs. Grose writes to him. On the walk to church one Sunday, Miles broaches the topic of school to the governess. He says he wants to go back and declares he will make his uncle come to Bly. The governess, shaken, does not go into church. Instead, she returns to the house and plots her departure. She sits on the bottom stair but springs up when she remembers seeing Miss Jessel there. She enters the schoolroom and finds Miss Jessel sitting at the table. She screams at the ghost, and the ghost vanishes. The governess decides she will stay at Bly. Mrs. Grose and the children return, saying nothing about the governess's absence at church. The governess agrees to write to her employer.

That evening, the governess listens outside Miles's door. He invites her in, and she questions him. She embraces him impulsively.

The candle goes out, and Miles shrieks. The next day Miles plays the piano for the governess. She suddenly realizes she doesn't know where Flora is. She and Mrs. Grose find Flora by the lake. There, the governess sees an apparition of Miss Jessel. She points it out to Flora and Mrs. Grose, but both claim not to see it. Flora says that the governess is cruel and that she wants to get away from her, and the governess collapses on the ground in hysterics. The next day, Mrs. Grose informs the governess that Flora is sick. They decide Mrs. Grose will take Flora to the children's uncle while the governess stays at Bly with Miles. Mrs. Grose informs the governess that Luke didn't send the letter she wrote to her employer, because he couldn't find it.

With Flora and Mrs. Grose gone, Miles and the governess talk after dinner. The governess asks if he took her letter. He confesses, and the governess sees Quint outside. She watches Quint in horror, then points him out to Miles, who asks if it is Peter Quint and looks out the window in vain. He cries out, then falls into the governess's arms, dead.

CHARACTER LIST

The Governess The protagonist of the novella, a twenty-year-old woman who has been put in charge of educating and supervising Flora and Miles at the country estate of Bly. The governess has had a very sheltered upbringing and little life experience, and her new job puts an immense responsibility on her, since she has no one to supervise or help her. She is intelligent as well as sensitive and emotionally volatile. Over the course of two short interviews with her employer, she fell in love with him, but she has no opportunity to see him or communicate with him. She is extremely protective of her charges and hopes to win her employer's approval. She views herself as a zealous guardian, a heroine facing dark forces. However, we never know for certain whether the ghosts and visions the governess sees are real or only figments of her imagination. No one else ever admits to seeing what she sees, and her fears, at times, seem to border on insanity.

Mrs. Grose A servant who acts as the governess's companion and confidante. Mrs. Grose, who is illiterate, is very aware of her low standing in comparison with the governess and treats the governess with great respect. Mrs. Grose listens patiently to the governess's constantly changing theories and insights, most often claiming to believe her but sometimes questioning whether the ghosts may not be imaginary. The governess, however, tends to overwhelm Mrs. Grose, often finishing Mrs. Grose's sentences or leaping to conclusions about what Mrs. Grose is saying. Thus, it can sometimes be difficult for us to judge whether Mrs. Grose is as strongly on the governess's side as the governess thinks. Mrs. Grose cares deeply about Flora and Miles and consistently defends them against the governess's accusations.

Miles A ten-year-old boy, the elder of the governess's two charges. Miles is charming and very attractive. He seems unnaturally well behaved and agreeable for a child, never fights with his sister, and tries constantly to please his governess. He is expelled from school for an unspecified but seemingly sinister reason, and although he seems to be a good child, he often hints that he is capable of being bad. The governess is alarmed by the fact that Miles never refers to his own past and suspects that wicked secrets belie his perfect exterior.

Flora An eight-year-old girl, the younger of the governess's two charges. Flora is beautiful and well mannered, a pleasure to be around. Although the governess loves Flora, she is disturbed that Flora, like Miles, seems strangely impersonal and reticent about herself. Flora is affectionate and always ready with an embrace or a smile. She is so unusually well behaved that her first instance of misconduct is disquieting. The governess eventually becomes convinced that Flora sees the ghost of Miss Jessel but keeps these sightings secret.

The Children's Uncle The governess's employer, a bachelor who lives in London. The uncle's attractiveness is one of the main reasons the governess agrees to take on her role at Bly. The uncle is friendly and pleasant, likely rich, and successful in charming women. He hires the governess on the condition that she handle his niece, nephew, and all problems at Bly herself. He asks not to be bothered about them.

Peter Quint A former valet at Bly. Red-haired, handsome, and exceedingly clever, Quint was "infamous" throughout the area of Bly. According to Mrs. Grose, he was a hound and "too free" with everyone, Miles and Flora included. The governess describes his specter as an unnaturally white, silent "horror." She believes Quint's ghost is haunting Bly with the intention of corrupting Miles.

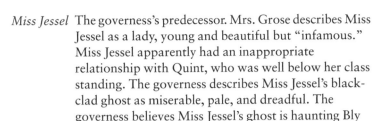

Miss Jessel The governess's predecessor. Mrs. Grose describes Miss Jessel as a lady, young and beautiful but "infamous." Miss Jessel apparently had an inappropriate relationship with Quint, who was well below her class standing. The governess describes Miss Jessel's black-clad ghost as miserable, pale, and dreadful. The governess believes Miss Jessel's ghost is haunting Bly with the intention of corrupting Flora.

Luke A servant at Bly. Luke is expected to deliver the governess's letter to the children's uncle, but he cannot find it. Miles uses Luke as an attempted escape route and asks to see Luke before telling the governess what she wants to know.

Anonymous Narrator The narrator of the prologue. The anonymous narrator is an educated guest at the Christmas Eve gathering. The narrator is most likely a man, since he speaks disdainfully of the sensation-hungry women at the gathering. The narrator may be a stand-in for Henry James, as he mentions he has a title for the tale at the end of the prologue. As Douglas repeatedly hints, the narrator will find a deeper meaning in the story.

Douglas The teller of the governess's tale at the Christmas Eve gathering. Douglas knew the governess, who had been his sister's governess after her time at Bly, and may have been in love with her. He is the only one who has heard the tale, since the governess left him in charge of her manuscript after she died. Douglas was fond of the governess and introduces her as a "most agreeable" person, giving her credibility regarding the tale to come.

Griffin A storyteller at the gathering. Griffin tells a ghost story involving a child and his mother.

Women at the Gathering Guests at the house. The women are characterized as sensation hungry and eager to hear the most "dreadful" and "delicious" ghost stories.

ANALYSIS OF MAJOR CHARACTERS

THE GOVERNESS

Although the governess adores Miles and Flora when she first meets them, she quickly becomes suspicious of their every word and action, convinced that they hope to deceive her. She is fickle, however, and frequently switches back to being absolutely sure of their pure innocence. At these times, her affection for the children can be intense. She embraces them often and with passion, going so far as to kiss Miles. The ambiguity of the text allows these displays of affection to appear both harmless and inappropriate. Her volatile relationship with the children renders her an unreliable narrator and a dubious source of information. According to Douglas, the governess's confidant and admirer, she is "the most agreeable person" he has ever known "in her position." However, he says also that she was "in love," as though this is an excuse for her behavior, which he admits is questionable. Mrs. Grose's increasing skepticism casts doubt on the governess's visions and fears and suggests that the governess may indeed be losing her mind.

The governess, with her overabundant concern for the children and her violent suspicions of them, may be regarded as either a heroine or a villain. On one hand, she seems to be an ambitious young woman who unwittingly places herself in a position in which she is forced to struggle heroically to protect her charges from supernatural forces. On the other hand, she seems to be a sheltered, inexperienced young woman whose crush on her employer and nervous exhaustion at being in charge of two strange children result in an elaborate and ultimately dangerous fabrication or hallucination. James provides only the governess's side of the story, which may be inaccurate in whole or in part. In any case, the governess's account is by no means the full account, which we never learn.

MRS. GROSE

An illiterate servant at Bly, Mrs. Grose provides the governess with open ears and loyal support. Although the governess thinks her simple minded and slow witted, Mrs. Grose knows more of the story than the governess fathoms and is as capable of piecing things together as is the governess, though slower to leap to dire conclusions. Although Mrs. Grose is the source for most of the governess's information, the governess does not take her words at face value or ask Mrs. Grose for her opinions. Instead, the governess uses Mrs. Grose as a "receptacle of lurid things." The governess frequently attempts to seize moments alone with Mrs. Grose so that she can try out her latest speculations. Mrs. Grose is usually skeptical of these speculations, but the governess takes Mrs. Grose's incredulity for astonished belief. Like the reader, Mrs. Grose is willing to hear the governess out but doesn't necessarily agree with her logic or conclusions.

MILES

Miles might be either a cunning and deceitful plaything of ghosts or merely an innocent, unusually well-mannered young boy. The governess repeatedly changes her mind on the matter, leaving Miles's true character in question. When the governess first meets Miles, she is struck by his "positive fragrance of purity" and the sense that he has known nothing but love. She finds herself excusing him for any potential mishap because he is too beautiful to misbehave. Yet she also senses a disturbing emptiness in Miles, an impersonality and lack of history, as though he is less than real.

Once the governess begins having her supernatural encounters, she comes to believe that Miles is plotting evil deeds with his ghostly counterpart, Quint, and indeed Miles does exhibit strange behavior. For example, he plans an incident so that the governess will think him "bad," and he steals the letter she wrote to his uncle. Mrs. Grose tells us that Peter Quint was a bad influence on him, but we have no way to measure the extent or precise nature of this influence, and Miles's misdeeds may be nothing more than childish pranks. The fact that Miles is otherwise unusually pleasant and well behaved suggests that the sinister quality of his behavior exists only in the governess's mind. The governess eventually decides that Miles must be full of wickedness, reasoning that he is too "exquisite" to be anything else, a conclusion she bases only on her own subjective impressions and conjectures.

FLORA

Like Miles, Flora might be either angelic or diabolical. She appears to be a completely wonderful little girl, even preternaturally so, well behaved and a pleasure to be around. The governess thinks Flora possesses "extraordinary charm" and is the "most beautiful child" she has laid eyes on. Flora seems, however, to have a personality quite distinct from these glowing descriptions. When the governess questions Flora as to why she had been looking out the window, Flora's explanation is evasive and unsatisfying. Flora's next turn at the window turns out to be, according to Miles, part of a scheme to show the governess that Miles can be "bad." At this point, the governess has already assumed Flora to be conniving and deceptive, but this is the first instance in which Flora seems to be exhibiting unambiguous deceit. The story remains inconclusive, however, and we never know for sure what Flora and Miles are up to. Flora may very well be the innocent child the governess thought her to be, her strange, diabolical turns existing only in the governess's mind.

Themes, Motifs, and Symbols

Themes

Themes are the fundamental and often universal ideas explored in a literary work.

The Corruption of the Innocent

The governess only rarely indicates that she is afraid the ghosts will physically harm or kill the children. In fact, Miles's death comes as a shock to us as readers, because we are unprepared to think of the ghosts as a physical threat. Until she sends Flora away, the governess never seems to consider removing the children from the ghosts or trying to expel the ghosts from the house. Instead, the governess's fears focus almost entirely on the potential "corruption" of the children—whether they were corrupted by Quint and Jessel when the latter were alive and whether they contiue to be similarly corrupted by the ghosts. Before she even knows about Quint, the governess guesses that Miles has been accused of corrupting other children. Although the word *corruption* is a euphemism that permits the governess to remain vague about what she means, the clear implication is that corruption means exposure to knowledge of sex. For the governess, the children's exposure to knowledge of sex is a far more terrifying prospect than confronting the living dead or being killed. Consequently, her attempt to save the children takes the form of a relentless quest to find out what they know, to make them confess rather than to predict what might happen to them in the future. Her fear of innocence being corrupted seems to be a big part of the reason she approaches the problem so indirectly—it's not just that the ghosts are unmentionable but that what the ghosts have said to them or introduced them to is unspeakable.

Because the corruption of the children is a matter of fearful speculation rather than an acknowledged fact, the story doesn't make any clear and definitive statement about corruption. Certainly, the governess's fears are destructive and do not result in her saving the children. Notably, while the governess is the character most fearful of and vigilant for corruption, she is also the least experienced and most curious character regarding sex. Mrs. Grose is married, and the uncle, though a bachelor, seems to be a ladies' man. The governess is singularly horrified by Miss Jessel's sexual infraction and apparently fascinated by it as well. We might conclude that the governess's fear of the children's corruption represents her projection of her own fears and desires regarding sex onto her charges.

THE DESTRUCTIVENESS OF HEROISM

The governess's youth and inexperience suggest that the responsibility of caring for the two children and being in charge of the entire estate is more than she could possibly bear, yet she does not look for help. Her isolation is largely her employer's fault, because he chooses to remain absent and specifically tells her to deal with all problems by herself. However, the governess responds to her experiences at Bly by taking on even more responsibility—to bury the headmaster's letter and keep Miles at home; to be the one who sees the ghosts rather than the children and who attempts to screen them from any exposure to the ghosts; and to save the children from the ghosts' corrupting influence. These decisions are all self-conscious—she is not forced to make them because she can't think of another way to respond. Instead, she deliberately chooses to view these challenges as "magnificent" opportunities to please the master and deludes herself into thinking that the master recognizes her sacrifices. Clearly, she is misguided on both counts. The master never comes down or sends any letter, and her crusade to save the children is an even worse disaster. Flora leaves the estate sick and in hysterics, vowing never to speak to the governess again, and Miles dies. Whether or not the governess was correct in thinking that the children were being haunted, she was definitely wrong in thinking she could be the hero who saves them.

The fact that the governess was misguided in adopting a heroic stance suggests several interpretations. One possibility is that the forces of corruption are too powerful for one person to oppose. Perhaps the governess could have succeeded only with the concerted efforts of the school and the uncle, and perhaps the children could not have been saved. Another possible reason why her heroism might have been inappropriate is that childhood and innocence may be too fragile to be protected in such an aggressive fashion. The governess's attempt to police and guard the children may have proven to be more damaging than the knowledge from which she wanted to protect them.

FORBIDDEN SUBJECTS

One of the most challenging features of *The Turn of the Screw* is how frequently characters make indirect hints or use vague language rather than communicate directly and clearly. The headmaster expels Miles from school and refuses to specify why. The governess has several guesses about what he might have done, but she just says he might be "corrupting" the others, which is almost as uninformative as the original letter. The governess fears that the children understand the nature of Quint and Jessel's relationship, but the nature of that relationship is never stated explicitly. The governess suspects that the ghosts are influencing the children in ways having to do with their relationship in the past, but she isn't explicit about how exactly they are being influenced. This excessive reticence on the part of the characters could reflect James's own reticence (which was marked), or it could be interpreted as a satiric reflection on Victorian reticence about sex. More straightforwardly, it could be a technique for engaging the imagination to produce a more terrifying effect.

MOTIFS

Motifs are recurring structures, contrasts, or literary devices that can help to develop and inform the text's major themes.

VISION

Throughout *The Turn of the Screw*, references to eyes and vision emphasize the idea that sight is unreliable. Vision and the language used to describe it are particularly important in each of the governess's encounters with Quint and Miss Jessel. She deems her first meeting with Quint a "bewilderment of vision," an ambiguous phrase that suggests she imagined what she saw. Characters lock eyes with each other several times in the novella. The governess shares intense gazes with both Quint and Miss Jessel and believes she can determine the ghosts' intentions by looking into their eyes. Although she and Miss Jessel do not actually talk, the governess claims Miss Jessel's gaze appears "to say" she has a right to be there. At times, the governess regards the clarity of the children's eyes as proof that the children are innocent. In these cases, she determines whether the children are capable of deception by looking at their eyes, when it may be her own eyes that deceive her.

A Ship Lost at Sea

Early on in the novella, the governess imagines herself at the helm of a "great drifting ship," and the metaphor of Bly as a ship lost at sea soon proves to be appropriate. When the governess goes out to look for the vanished Quint, she describes Bly as "empty with a great emptiness," as though it is a vast, unlimited sea. After her first ghostly encounters, she decides she will save the children but later cries that they are hopelessly "lost." Her navigation skills have failed her, and she envisions the children drowning. However, she perseveres, and when she speaks with Miles near the end of the novel, she feels she is "just nearly reaching port." The ship imagery extends further when, soon thereafter, she imagines Miles "at the bottom of the sea," a disturbing image that foreshadows Miles's fate. Ultimately, the governess is the character who is most lost. She cannot find a direction or destination for her theories and suspicions, and her perceptions are constantly changing.

Silence

Sound acts as a signal of life and nature in *The Turn of the Screw*, and its absence is a predictor of the governess's supernatural visions. Prior to the governess's ghostly encounters, she experiences a hush in the world around her. When she first sees Quint in the tower, the sound of birds stops and the rustling of leaves quiets. The governess takes the scene to be "stricken with death." Nothing else changes, however, and the visual aspects of the world around her are unaffected. The governess's sense of a hush is more marked when she meets Quint on the staircase. She interprets the "dead silence" of the incident as proof that the encounter is unnatural. In fact, she remarks that the silence is the specific thing that marks the event as unnatural and that otherwise she would have assumed Quint to be a living being. Quint's subsequent disappearance into silence suggests that the dead dwell in a realm without sound, making silence a mark of the unnatural and unliving.

SYMBOLS

Symbols are objects, characters, figures, or colors used to represent abstract ideas or concepts.

LIGHT

Candlelight suggests safety in the governess's narrative, while twilight suggests danger. On a number of occasions, the governess's lighted candle is extinguished, always with the implication that something is awry. At the top of the stairs, her candle goes out at the exact moment she sees Quint. She views him in "cold, faint twilight." A week or two later, the governess wakes up to find her candle extinguished and Miles on the lawn in bright moonlight. Her view of him in that light suggests danger and, in a way, prefigures his imminent death. Later, Miles blows out the governess's candle, plunging the two into darkness. The lack of moonlight implies an absence of the supernatural, and the blowing out of the candle indicates a loss of protection.

THE WRITTEN WORD

In *The Turn of the Screw*, events become fully real only when they have been written down. The governess at first refuses to record the circumstances at Bly in a letter to her employer. If she preserves the events in a material document, she will have reached a point of no return—she will be forever unable to deny what happened. She also has relied on threats and passionate speech to persuade Mrs. Grose of her visions and theories, and convincing someone through the written word will be much more difficult. Eventually, she does write the letter, and she also writes down the entire account in the manuscript that we are reading. The manuscript, unlike the letter, allows her to present events in a way that will persuade her readers she is both sane and telling the truth. In keeping with the ambiguity of the tale, the trajectories of both written records, the letter and the manuscript, are interrupted, which further impedes our ability to determine whether the events are or are not "real." The letter is never sent, and the manuscript stops short of a definite conclusion. These interruptions suggest the story remains unresolved—and cast doubt on its reliability.

Summary and Analysis

Prologue and Chapter I

Summary: Prologue

An unnamed narrator describes a house party at which ghost stories are told. The guests agree that a story in which a ghost visits a child is especially eerie, and an older guest named Douglas indicates that he knows a story in which a ghost visits *two* children. Everyone present wants to hear the story, but Douglas insists that he has to send his servant to his house in London to get it, as the story is in written form, penned many years earlier by Douglas's sister's governess, with whom Douglas was apparently infatuated.

The manuscript arrives, and Douglas provides some background before reading it to the party. When the young woman who wrote the manuscript was twenty years old and just finished with her education, she answered an advertisement for a position as governess. The employer was a rich, attractive bachelor responsible for educating his orphaned niece and nephew, who lived at his remote country house. The position was isolated and lonely, and the bachelor stipulated that she must deal with all problems by herself and never seek to correspond with him. Nevertheless, the young woman accepted the position, perhaps because of her attraction to her employer.

Summary: Chapter I

The governess's narrative opens with her drive to Bly, a country home in Essex, a county in eastern England. Here she meets the housekeeper, Mrs. Grose, and the younger of her two charges, Flora, an exceptionally beautiful and charming little girl. From her room, the governess thinks she hears the footsteps and crying of a child in the distance but dismisses them, optimistic about the opportunity to teach and shape her beautiful charge.

Talking with Mrs. Grose, the governess asks about Flora's brother. Mrs. Grose emphasizes the boy's good looks, and the governess remarks impulsively upon her employer's handsomeness. Mrs. Grose tells the governess that Flora's brother will arrive on Friday, at which the governess decides that she and Flora will meet him together. She spends the entire next day with Flora, who shows the new governess her home with delight. Summing up her feelings in retrospect, the governess expresses her then-optimistic attitude toward her new position in contrast to her present feelings toward Bly as "ugly," a drifting ship of which she herself was at the helm.

ANALYSIS

By the time we finish the prologue and begin the governess's narrative, we know that the story to come is a ghost story and that it involves a governess who is in love with her employer. Ordinarily, given this basic story premise, we would expect the story to be a gothic romance and to have an unrealistic plot, primarily in the sense that it would contain supernatural elements but also in the idea that a governess might aspire to rise above her station and win the love of a rich gentleman—something that happens in gothic romances such as *Jane Eyre* but not in real life. In other words, to read a story like this, we would normally be prepared to put aside our cynicism about whether these events could actually happen and simply enjoy the story. The main function of the prologue, however, is to tell us *not* to do this.

The prologue depicts an audience for the governess's story that is adult, worldly, and cynical rather than naïve or sentimental. The narrator makes it clear that some of the guests are more sophisticated than others and that those who remain to hear Douglas's story are a select group. This group is characterized as "arch," meaning deliberately or even forcedly ironic and playful. The group's members are fairly aggressive about reading between the lines of what Douglas says to draw sexual inferences, as Mrs. Griffin does about Douglas and the governess. The guest who wisecracks about the former governess dying of "so much respectability" is insinuating that the former governess is less than respectable, perhaps morally and sexually loose. This guest treats Douglas's story skeptically, even cynically, refusing to take things at face value and ready to make inferences of a sexual nature. When we learn more about this former governess—Miss Jessel—we see that this guest is absolutely right and perhaps conclude that we are intended to read *The Turn of the Screw* in the same way: viewing the characters realistically rather than romantically, treating the story skeptically, and reading between the lines for sexual overtones.

From the first sentence of her narrative, in Chapter I, the governess calls attention to her own sharp swings in mood and attitude, a focus that makes her seem sensitive, emotional, nervous, and introspective but not necessarily reliable. Her perceptions of things at Bly are clearly shaped by her emotions and her imagination, and often her judgments seem excessively hasty or intense. Her reaction to Flora, in particular, seems excessive, as she describes Flora in such idealized terms ("radiant," "beatific") that we get little sense of Flora as a real child. The governess feels affection for Mrs. Grose, but her feelings often change quickly, though briefly, to suspeicion. The governess reports hearing footsteps and crying outside her room, and she gets the sense that Mrs. Grose is *too* glad to see her, both of which provide foreshadowing and create the sense that something is going on that we have yet to learn about. However, the governess's sensitivity and volatility also create a feeling of uncertainty about whether we can trust her point of view. This question is one of the central problems of *The Turn of the Screw*, and it develops and deepens rather than resolves.

> *[. . .] I had the fancy of our being almost as lost as a handful of passengers in a great drifting ship. Well, I was, strangely, at the helm!*
>
> *(See* QUOTATIONS, *p. 42)*

CHAPTERS II AND III

SUMMARY: CHAPTER II

Together with Flora, the governess drives out to meet Miles. The governess is unsettled by a letter from her employer that came in the mail on her first day. Enclosed was another letter, from Miles's headmaster, saying that Miles is no longer welcome at school. Distressed by the thought that Miles might be a troublemaker and the knowledge that she has agreed to tend to matters herself, she questions Mrs. Grose. Her companion, as distressed as she, seems not to understand why Miles had been turned out from school.

The governess later that day approaches her colleague again, asking Mrs. Grose if she has ever known Miles to cause trouble. Mrs. Grose implies that Miles had on occasion been bad, but that was to be expected from a boy. A few hours before leaving to meet Miles, the governess approaches Mrs. Grose once more, questioning her about the previous governess. Mrs. Grose describes her as young and pretty but is evasive about her death, claiming she does not know why the young woman died.

SUMMARY: CHAPTER III

The governess is late picking up Miles, whom she finds standing outside the inn exuding the same beauty and purity as Flora. Joining Mrs. Grose back at Bly, the governess rejects, on the basis of Miles's attractive appearance, any charges she or the headmaster may have made against Miles. She determines to do nothing in regard to Miles's expulsion. Mrs. Grose says she will stand by that decision, and the two kiss and embrace. The governess soon becomes absorbed in her responsibilities, and her two pupils give her little, if any, trouble.

During her private hour one evening, the governess takes a walk around the grounds, fantasizing unrealistically about meeting her master, and when she comes back in view of the house she sees a strange man standing atop one of the house's towers, looking at her. The governess experiences a stillness and sudden hush. Her confrontation with the man lasts a long, intense moment before he passes from one of the tower's corners to the other. In retrospect, the governess remembers that the man turned away from her without ever breaking his stare.

ANALYSIS

Chapter II introduces the tantalizing mystery of what Miles did to get himself expelled from school. Although Miles looks like an angel and was one of the youngest boys there, he apparently did something so bad that the school didn't think disciplining him would be sufficient, possibly because he poses some kind of danger to the other students. Strangely, the headmaster refuses to even mention in the letter what Miles did. Since James never lets us know what happened, we might conclude that guessing the answer is impossible—that James never had something specific in mind and instead leaves Miles's crime to our imaginations to create a sinister impression. If, on the other hand, we decide that an answer to this riddle exists and that we are supposed to read between the lines to figure it out, then the crime would have to be *both* something that was condemned by Victorian society *and* something that there was a taboo against speaking about. To many of us, these facts suggest strongly that Miles's infraction was sexual in nature. As we see in subsequent chapters, he may have been exposed to sex by unscrupulous former servants, and thus he may be imparting knowledge about sex to his peers at school or perhaps engaging in sexual behaviors. (In Chapter XXIV, he finally admits that he "said things" to people he "liked" and that those people repeated the things he said to those *they* liked.) His infraction might involve knowledge of heterosexual acts, masturbation, or homosexuality—it is impossible to know for certain.

The governess's reaction to the headmaster's letter is both odd and revealing. A more practical governess might follow up with the school, make persistent inquiries, obtain actual facts, and try to resolve the situation. Instead, this governess lets her imagination run wild, conjuring up the darkest possibilities, hinting at the sexual nature of his misdeed when she refers to the possibility of his corrupting the other students. Despite her curiosity and ability to imagine horrible scenarios, she avoids pursuing the facts. She seems to want the situation to be complicated and difficult rather than simple, apparently because she wants a heroic challenge that gives her the opportunity to win the gratitude of the absent employer with whom she's in love.

Chapter III features the first supernatural event, the governess's first sighting of the ghost of Peter Quint—though neither we nor the governess realize he's a ghost until the end of Chapter V. To put this scene in perspective, it is important to know that one of the most debated questions of *The Turn of the Screw* is whether the ghosts are real or whether the governess hallucinates them—and if she hallucinates them, why she does so. The reasons for suspecting the governess of hallucinating come later in the story, when the governess behaves more erratically and her understanding of the situation seems more questionable. At this point in the story, we don't have much reason to question what the governess sees. In fact, we are likely to continue thinking that the ghosts are real and resist the idea that the governess is insane precisely because it seems impossible that the governess could have imagined the ghost, since she sees Peter Quint before she has even heard of him.

However, Peter Quint's appearance is not quite as random as it seems. In Chapter II, Mrs. Grose inadvertently alludes to Peter Quint without mentioning his name, saying that he liked his girls young and pretty, and the governess picks up on this slip, asking whom Mrs. Grose means, since it is obviously not the master. This exchange could be seen as simple foreshadowing, but perhaps also as the planting of the idea in the governess's mind that a strange and sexually predatory man is somehow associated with Bly. Another fact worth noting about Quint is that before the governess sees him, she is fantasizing about running into someone—perhaps her employer—during her walk. If we decide to look for evidence that

Quint is a hallucination rather than a ghost, the fact that Quint's appearance is so closely tied to the governess's desire for the master might serve as the basis for a psychological interpretation. The governess's mind may have produced Quint both as a substitute object of sexual desire and as a further pretext for heroism that will please her employer.

CHAPTERS IV AND V

SUMMARY: CHAPTER IV

Confused, the governess wonders what sort of mystery Bly might hold. Meeting Mrs. Grose at the house, she points to the evening's beauty as her reason for staying out so late. For days, the governess reflects on her encounter with the intruder. Meanwhile, her time spent with Miles and Flora goes smoothly. Still wondering about the cause of the boy's expulsion, she decides finally that he was too refined for the "horrid, unclean school-world" and had been punished for it. As much as the governess enjoys her charges, she is concerned that both children are impersonal, seemingly without history.

One Sunday, the governess comes down the stairs to meet Mrs. Grose for church, only to meet a disturbing visage at the window. It is the intruder from the tower, staring intensely at her from outside the dining-room window. The governess runs outside to confront the man, but he has vanished. She turns to the window to stand where he had stood. At that moment, Mrs. Grose enters the dining room and is startled by the image of the governess staring in from outside.

SUMMARY: CHAPTER V

Mrs. Grose, breathless, asks the governess why she looks so frightened. The governess responds by saying she cannot go to church and claims that what Mrs. Grose saw was not half as bad as what she herself saw just a few moments ago. She then bewilders and frightens her colleague by detailing her experience with the intruder at the window and, earlier, at the tower. Calling the man "a horror," the governess tells Mrs. Grose that she feels compelled to stay and watch their home instead of going to church. Mrs. Grose asks what the man looked like, and the governess describes him as without a hat, with very red hair and a pale face. Mrs. Grose suddenly makes an expression of recognition and names the intruder as Peter Quint, her employer's former valet. At the governess's questioning, Mrs. Grose reveals that Quint was in charge of Bly last year until his death.

ANALYSIS

The governess's first thoughts after seeing Peter Quint are to compare her situation to the plots of two popular gothic novels with romantic heroines, Ann Radcliffe's *The Mysteries of Udolpho* and Charlotte Brontë's *Jane Eyre*—the latter about a governess who marries her employer, which we know to be this governess's fantasy. However, the effect of these references is not to make the governess's story seem more like those novels, but just the opposite. The fact that she is inclined to see herself in terms of these gothic romances reminds us that this is *not* a romance; that those are fantasies rather than reality; and that even though we know that what we are reading is a work of fiction, it's a work of realistic fiction.

The governess's second sighting of Peter Quint, as he stares in through the window, differs from the first in that it is slightly more subjective. Her description of the first sighting focuses exclusively on what Quint looks like and what she sees him do, but this time she reports being seized by a flash of insight and certain knowledge that Quint is looking for someone other than her. This difference is important because the governess's claims about the ghosts become increasingly more subjective as the story goes on. By Chapter VI, she claims to know that Quint was looking for Miles. We believe the governess because her first vision seems to be very factual—she observes a man, she doesn't know he is a ghost, and she doesn't know he looks like Quint; therefore, her vision must be trustworthy. As we read further, however, the governess claims to know or intuit many things that cannot be proven simply by the evidence of her senses. The less factual her impressions, the less certain we are that she is trustworthy. When Mrs. Grose sees the governess peering in from the spot where Quint was, she describes the governess as a terrifying and dreadful sight, hinting that the governess herself may be a source of terror to others rather than a hero or savior, as the governess would like to think.

The governess's description for Mrs. Grose of Peter Quint's appearance displays a strange mixture of attraction and repulsion. Even if we feel sure that Quint is a real ghost and not a product of the governess's mind, we may still get the sense that the governess's perceptions about Quint are not purely insightful and that, to a certain extent, the governess projects her own desires and fears onto him. Quint is clearly a foil for the absent master—similarly attractive, and at one time the master's proxy at Bly, but emphatically not a gentleman like the master. We know that the governess fell in love with the master during their interviews, so we can assume that the master awakened sexual desires in the governess. However, the governess has no outlet for those feelings, because the precondition for winning the master's approval is to endure his absence and not seek to communicate with him. She describes Quint as "tall, active, erect" and "remarkably" handsome, making it clear that she finds him attractive, but she also perceives him as aggressive and terrifying. We might infer that her frustrated desire for the master is what prompts her to see Quint as a sexual substitute, as someone who is attractive but, unlike the master, available. However, Quint's sexual availability is also terrifying, because the social consequences of sex with a man like him would be so destructive. The governess's fear of Quint's sexuality (or her fear of her own desire for him) seems to manifest itself as a contempt for his status as a servant, and throughout the story she dwells on the dangers and evils of his lower-class, servile, ungentlemanly condition.

CHAPTERS VI, VII, AND VIII

SUMMARY: CHAPTER VI
The governess and Mrs. Grose discuss the governess's encounter with what they assume to be the ghost of Peter Quint. With a feeling of sudden clarity, the governess exclaims that Quint had been looking for Miles. She wonders why neither child has ever mentioned the man. Mrs. Grose reveals that Quint had been "too free" with Miles. Still haunted by the image of Peter Quint, the governess sleeps fitfully, if at all, and remains convinced Mrs. Grose has left out some important detail.

The governess begins to view the situation as an occasion for heroism and zealously takes up the role as protector of Miles and Flora. Later, with Miles inside, the governess watches Flora play on the bank of the lake when she becomes aware of a third presence. The governess turns her eyes to Flora, who is attempting to build a small wooden boat and seems oblivious to any sort of irregularity. The governess then shifts her eyes in the direction of their visitor.

SUMMARY: CHAPTER VII
The narrative moves forward to later that afternoon, when the governess informs Mrs. Grose of the encounter. She claims that the children "know" and are keeping things to themselves, explaining that

Flora saw a woman at the lake but said nothing. The governess describes the vision as dressed in black, with a dreadful face, and says the woman appeared out of nowhere. Responding to Mrs. Grose's questions, the governess claims the woman is Miss Jessel, her predecessor, and that she is certain Flora will lie about it. Mrs. Grose defends Flora as innocent, then inquires further. The governess says Miss Jessel "fixed" Flora with determined eyes and remarks on Miss Jessel's beauty. At this, Mrs. Grose speaks of Miss Jessel as "infamous" and reveals that Miss Jessel had an inappropriate relationship with Quint. Clinging to Mrs. Grose in distress, the governess laments that the children are lost beyond her control.

SUMMARY: CHAPTER VIII

Meeting again later, the governess and Mrs. Grose determine to keep their wits about them. That night they talk in the governess's room until the governess is convinced that Mrs. Grose believes her. The governess returns to her pupils and feels ashamed at having thought Flora capable of cunning. Later, she asks Mrs. Grose about the occasions on which Miles had been bad. It takes prying, but Mrs. Grose finally tells her that her previous reference had regarded the time Miles had spent with Quint. Mrs. Grose defends Miles, pointing out that Miss Jessel had not disapproved of his and Quint's relationship. Getting fed up with the governess's relentless questioning, Mrs. Grose fires back some retorts. The governess pieces together her colleague's revelations and presumes that Mrs. Grose's silence signifies her agreement. Mrs. Grose confirms that whenever Miles had been with Quint, Flora had been with Miss Jessel. As Mrs. Grose again defends Miles, the governess reassures her that without more evidence, she can accuse no one and will simply wait.

ANALYSIS

In these chapters, as the governess learns about Quint and Jessel and their relationship with the children, her views toward them evolve from the idea that the ghosts are trying to get at the children and that she can shield them to suspecting that the children are already under the ghosts' influence and are corrupted, and thus need to be even more vigorously watched and more aggressively rescued. From this point on, everything the children say or do may be duplicitous and ironic. Even if we believe that the ghosts are real, we don't know whether the governess is right about the children. Her assertions that the children are aware of the ghosts are based on subjective impressions and intuitions, not on clear visual evidence. Moreover, the governess's interpretation of events at Bly is opportunistic, even self-serving. She sees the problem of the ghosts and the chance to save the children as a "magnificent opportunity," a chance to fulfill her fantasy of winning the master's approval through an act of heroism.

The nature of the children's relationship with Quint and Jessel is only hinted at, and it can be interpreted in different ways. We know from Mrs. Grose that Miles spent a lot of time with Quint, despite Mrs. Grose's disapproval of a servant and master being so friendly. We also gather that Quint was "too free" with Miles and everyone else, that Quint and Jessel had an affair, and that Quint did what he liked with people. All of these statements are vague and ambiguous. Seen in the most positive light, Mrs. Grose's account can be interpreted to mean merely that Quint was a bad influence on Miles because of his lower-class manners. At worst, Mrs. Grose's words might imply that Quint exposed Miles to sexual knowledge by telling him about sex, by letting Miles witness him having sex, or even by having sex with Miles. Similarly, Mrs. Grose's assertion that Quint was "free" with everyone and did what he liked with people could mean merely that he was rude and spoke to people however he wanted, or it could mean that he seduced or sexually abused the other servants. The governess is quick to interpret the situation in a sexual way, insisting that Miles and Flora understood the true nature of Quint and Jessel's relationship and that they helped to cover it up. She sees the situation as much worse than does Mrs. Grose, perceiving herself as bolder and more willing to face the truth than Mrs. Grose. We don't know the truth for certain, and our sense that there are no limits to how bad the situation might be creates a feeling of vertigo and terror in us.

In Chapter VIII, Mrs. Grose raises the idea that the governess might have imagined the ghosts, and the governess silences her by pointing out that she described each ghost down to the last detail and that Mrs. Grose identified them by these descriptions. The validity of this argument is ambiguous, however. This might be a fair description of how they identify Peter Quint, but in the case of Miss Jessel, not only does the governess not provide a detailed description, *she* is the one who asserts that the woman in black was Miss Jessel. This discrepancy is definitely noteworthy, giving us some reason to mistrust the governess, but it doesn't settle the question one way or the other, because the governess's point still seems valid as applied to Quint.

CHAPTERS IX, X, XI, XII, AND XIII

SUMMARY: CHAPTER IX

Days pass without incident. The governess keeps the children under her constant supervision. She finds herself embracing her pupils more frequently and with sharper passion, and she wonders if they are aware of her suspicions. Likewise, the two children become increasingly fond of their governess and seek to please her as much and as often as possible. The governess questions whether an ulterior motive exists in their newly amplified affection.

The lull is broken one night when the governess is startled from her nighttime reading. After quietly rising from her bed, she leaves the room and moves to the top of the staircase. Suddenly her candle goes out, and she witnesses an apparition of Quint halfway up the stairway. They stare each other down intensely, the governess refusing to back down. She is convinced by the dead silence that the vision is "unnatural." She watches as the figure disappears.

SUMMARY: CHAPTER X

A moment later, the governess returns to her room to find that Flora is not in her bed, but the bed's curtains have been pulled forward. The governess is distraught but soon notices a movement behind the window blind. From under it Flora emerges with a grave expression. Flora reproaches the governess, asking where she has been. The governess explains her absence, then questions Flora, who says she could sense the governess had left and thought someone was walking out in the grounds. According to Flora, no one was outside. The governess is certain Flora is lying and questions her further about the drawn bed curtains. Flora claims she hadn't wanted to frighten the governess, who could have returned at any moment.

Henceforth, the governess stays up most nights. One evening she finds the apparition of Miss Jessel with her head in her hands at the bottom of the stairs. The vision vanishes immediately. A number of evenings pass without event. The night that she finally decides it is safe to sleep at her normal hour, she awakens after midnight to find her light out. Certain Flora has extinguished it, she gets out of bed and finds her student at the window. The governess decides Flora must be communicating with the ghost of Miss Jessel and, careful not to disturb her, ventures out to find a room with a window that looks on the same scene. There, from her window, the governess sees Miles out on the lawn.

SUMMARY: CHAPTER XI

The next day, as the children stroll together on the lawn under supervision, the governess informs Mrs. Grose of Miles's misconduct. The governess tells Mrs. Grose what passed between her and Miles after she had found him outside in the moonlight. When she had appeared on the lawn, he had promptly come to her, and she had led him inside without a word. The governess had then questioned Miles as to what he had been doing. Smiling, Miles had explained that he had wanted her to think him capable of being "bad." Then he had kissed her and gone into further detail about his plan. According to Miles, he had arranged things with Flora to disturb the governess, so she would then get up to find out what was going on. He had been delighted that she had fallen for it and expressed pride in being "bad enough." The two had ended their conversation with an embrace.

SUMMARY: CHAPTER XII

Mrs. Grose is nonplussed by the governess's account, and so the governess explains her conclusion that the children have been meeting consistently with Quint and Miss Jessel. She goes so far as to claim that as the children stroll, they are "talking horrors" and plotting their next meeting with their two ghostly friends. The governess, piecing things together, says that the children have not been good but empty, and their lives belong to Quint and Miss Jessel. Furthermore, the governess surmises, Quint and Miss Jessel "want to get" the children to destroy them and keep up their diabolical work. Mrs. Grose suggests that the governess write to her employer, asking him to take the children away. The governess rejects that idea, saying he will think her mad. Mrs. Grose throws out an alternative plan for the governess to make her employer come to her. At this, the governess foresees his amusement and derision at what he will perceive to be her loneliness. She threatens to leave if Mrs. Grose appeals to the children's uncle on her behalf.

SUMMARY: CHAPTER XIII

The governess believes that the children are aware that she knows about their relationships with Quint and Miss Jessel. When together, she and the children avoid any subject that nears forbidden territory, and she finds herself repeatedly recalling events in her personal history to fill conversational space. The season changes to autumn. As day after day passes without incident, the governess thinks perhaps her eyes have been sealed and that the children are communicating with unseen visitors in her very presence. Even so, her charges are more likeable each day.

Unable to broach the topic of Quint and Miss Jessel with the children, the governess shuts herself up in a room to rehearse. Still, in their company, she cannot find the nerve and instead finds herself chattering more than ever, always until she notices a sudden, strange silence. These perceived stillnesses have become common when she is with her pupils, but all three refuse to acknowledge that they occur. The children begin to ask the governess about their uncle and why he hasn't visited or written. The governess has the children write letters to him with the understanding that such writings are merely educational exercises.

ANALYSIS

These chapters detail the governess's struggle to protect and save the children, together with her growing impression that the children are deceiving her and that things are worse than she thought. Although she does see Quint and Jessel again, most of the suspense is now generated by what she suspects and imagines about the children's dealings with the ghosts. She no longer fears confronting the ghosts but instead fears that she has lost the power to see them and that the ghosts are appearing to the children in her very presence, telling them something infernal or referring to "dreadful passages of intercourse in the past." Now the terror is purely psychological, and we are drawn in to share her fears because, just like her, there seems to be something terrible going on that we also can't define.

We see things from the governess's point of view, and the children appear to be a mixture of things—charming, affectionate, angelic, and wonderfully tactful but also duplicitous and subtle. We are given much less information about how the children may perceive the governess, but that which we are given is rather unsettling. The governess describes her own behavior as both extremely vigilant and watchful and extremely affectionate—she perpetually bows down and hugs the children. Yet her expressions of affection and her constant surveillance have oppressive and suffocating overtones, and there are hints that the children tolerate rather than welcome it. In moments of crisis, the governess seems downright frightening. Thinking Flora has lied, the governess grips her in a "spasm" and reports being surprised that Flora does not cry out in surprise or fright. When she questions Miles, she is aware of answering him "only with a vague repeated grimacing nod." She always suppresses her urge to ask about the ghosts but instead cross-examines the children about what they say and do. If the children are innocent and do not see the ghosts, the governess's behavior must seem strange and terrifying.

CHAPTERS XIV, XV, XVI, AND XVII

SUMMARY: CHAPTER XIV
The governess walks to church accompanied by Miles. Mrs. Grose and Flora are ahead of them, on their way to church as well. On the way, Miles brings up school, asking when he will be going back. He quickly adds that he has grown tired of always being around women and points out that he has been very well behaved, except for that one night. The governess interviews Miles carefully, trying to coax out of him the reason for his expulsion from school. She is unsuccessful. Miles maintains that he wants to go back to school to be around his "own sort," to which the governess laughs and refers to Flora as the only example of his "sort" she knows. Nearing the gate for church, Miles asks whether his uncle agrees with the governess on the matter, and the governess tells Miles she doesn't think his uncle cares about his situation. Triumphantly declaring that he will make his uncle come to Bly and care, Miles marches off into church alone.

SUMMARY: CHAPTER XV
The governess turns away from church, feeling defeated by Miles and taken aback by the sudden revelation that he possesses "consciousness and a plan." With the sudden intention of leaving Bly, she returns to the house and impulsively sits at the bottom of the staircase. She jumps up quickly, repulsed by the memory that the spot is the same place where Miss Jessel had sat during their last encounter. The governess heads for the schoolroom, where she finds Miss Jessel at the table, in the same position as before, with her head in her hands. The ghost rises with an air of indifference to the governess's entrance. Standing not far from the governess, Miss Jessel stares intently at her. The governess is disturbed by the feeling that she is the one who is intruding and cries out to the ghost, calling her a "terrible, miserable woman." Miss Jessel looks at the governess as though she understands, then vanishes. The room is now empty and bright with sunshine, and the governess has a strong feeling that she must stay on at Bly.

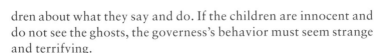

SUMMARY & ANALYSIS

SUMMARY: CHAPTER XVI

Mrs. Grose and the two children return home from church and act as though the governess's absence is nothing unusual. The governess, hurt and upset, manages to get Mrs. Grose alone so that she can inquire as to whether the children "bribed her to silence." Mrs. Grose confirms the governess's suspicion, saying the children had asked her not to say anything. She says the children told her that the governess would be happier if they made no mention of it and that they must do all they can to please her. The governess tells Mrs. Grose that everything is "all out" between Miles and her, and she goes on to say that she has had "a talk" with Miss Jessel. When Mrs. Grose inquires further, the governess claims that Miss Jessel spoke of the torments of the dead and that the ghost wants Flora.

To Mrs. Grose's relief, the governess says she will send for the children's uncle. The two discuss the problem of Miles's expulsion, with the governess deciding that the reason was "wickedness." Mrs. Grose defends Miles, saying his relationship with Quint was not his fault and that she will take the blame. Mrs. Grose then offers to write to the uncle instead. The governess responds with sarcasm, asking her colleague if she wants to write out their fantastical story. Breaking down with tears in her eyes, Mrs. Grose entreats the governess to write the letter. The governess says she will write that evening, and the two separate.

SUMMARY: CHAPTER XVII

The governess begins writing to the children's uncle that windy evening. Restless, she gets up to listen at Miles's door. Miles calls out for her to come in, saying he heard her walk across the passage. When the governess enters his room, Miles brings up the "queer business" of how the governess is bringing him up. Holding her breath, the governess asks what he means, to which he replies that she knows. She tells him he will go back to school and points out that she hadn't known his desire to return because he had never spoken of it. Miles ponders and asks, "[H]aven't I?" His expression triggers a pang in the governess. She confirms that no, he has never mentioned any detail about school, and she had always assumed that he was happy at Bly.

Miles shakes his head and says he wants to "get away." When the governess asks him to clarify, he replies "[Y]*ou* know what a boy wants!" He rejects the idea of going to his uncle's but declares that his uncle must come to Bly and settle things. At this, the governess begins to question Miles about things he hasn't told her. Miles asserts that he wants a different environment with such serenity that the governess throws herself onto him with embraces. Miles lets her kiss him, then tells her to "let [him] alone." The governess again tries to pry from him the reason for his expulsion. At his "quaver of consenting consciousness," she embraces him again, when with a chilly gust, the room turns dark and Miles shrieks. The governess exclaims that the candle has gone out, and Miles says that it was he who blew it out.

ANALYSIS

These chapters represent a struggle between Miles and the governess, as he challenges her to send him back to school or justify why she has not. Miles clearly wants freedom from the governess's scrutiny and control, but we do not know exactly why he wants this freedom. We read page after page of the governess's fears and conjectures, but the actual lines of dialogue from the other three characters are very few and almost absurdly cryptic and ambiguous. What Miles says he wants seems on the surface to be utterly ordinary, but in the context of the governess's fears and suspicions, his words seem ominous and fraught with double meanings. For example, he says that he wants to be "with his own sort" and that the governess knows what boys want, words that could be innocent and banal or salacious. He may mean he wants to be around other boys, or he may be making a coded reference to his homosexuality. James seems to tease us by suggesting that whatever we see in this story reveals more about us and our preoccupations than it does about the story itself. Possibly, the characters' cryptic statements and vague suggestions of double entendres may be intended to satirize Victorian reticence about sexual matters.

Miles gains a psychological advantage over the governess when he tells her he will convince his uncle to come down and discuss his schooling, and the governess is too overcome with agitation at hearing this to go to church. The governess explains to the reader that she is worried about having to deal with the painful subject of Miles's expulsion with the uncle, but it is possible that her agitation has more to do with her attraction to the uncle. Thus far, she has sublimated her feelings for her employer, pouring them into her effort to rescue the children and to shield the employer from any trouble. At the end of Chapter XIII, she even asserts that his complete silence is intended to flatter and pay tribute to her. The idea of confronting the employer face to face has become quite alarming for her, and her experiences after she leaves the children at the church door suggest that she feels guilty about her desires. The best evidence for her feelings of guilt is when she begins to identify herself with Miss Jessel, whom she now sees as the most odious woman possible because Miss Jessel had had a sexual affair. First, she is upset when she realizes she has collapsed on the bottom step of the staircase exactly as Miss Jessel had sat earlier. Then, she sees Miss Jessel at her own writing desk and assumes her to be a servant writing a love letter—Miss Jessel is apparently using the governess's own pens to do something that the governess herself would like to do but cannot. Finally, she decides that Miss Jessel is asserting that she has just as much right to be there as the governess. Miss Jessel apparently represents something that the governess simultaneously identifies with, desires, and loathes.

CHAPTERS XVIII, XIX, XX, AND XXI

SUMMARY: CHAPTER XVIII

The next day Mrs. Grose asks the governess if she has written the letter. The governess affirms this but does not mention that the letter has not yet been sent. That morning her pupils perform brilliantly at their tasks. After dinner, Miles approaches the governess to ask if she would like him to play the piano for her. She is delighted, and he plays remarkably for some time, until the governess realizes the length of time that has passed and realizes that Flora is nowhere to be seen. She asks Miles where his sister is. He asks how he should know and laughs.

To no avail, the governess searches for Flora in her bedroom upstairs and in other rooms downstairs. She then looks for Mrs. Grose, but Flora is not with her, nor is she with the maids. The governess has a feeling that Flora is "at a distance" and insinuates the she must be with Miss Jessel. Horrified, Mrs. Grose asks where Miles is. The governess deduces he is with Quint in the schoolroom. She then declares that "the trick's played" and informs Mrs. Grose that Miles had distracted her. Mrs. Grose asks about the letter, and the governess draws it from her pocket and leaves it on the table for a servant named Luke to take. Although Mrs. Grose is loathe to leave Miles, the governess persuades her to accompany her outside to search for Flora.

SUMMARY: CHAPTER XIX

The governess and Mrs. Grose head to the lake, the governess convinced that Flora has fled to where she had seen the image of Miss Jessel. Flora is neither there nor seen on the opposite bank. The governess determines that Flora must have taken the boat, which is missing from its usual resting place. She leads Mrs. Grose to the other side of the lake. Soon they find the boat and shortly thereafter come upon Flora, who is smiling.

Flora plucks a spray of fern and waits for the governess and Mrs. Grose to approach. As Mrs. Grose embraces Flora passionately, Flora glances at the governess from over Mrs. Grose's shoulder with a grave expression. Mrs. Grose lets the child go. Flora speaks first, asking where their "things" are, as they are all without hats. She then asks where Miles is. The governess says she will tell her if Flora will tell the governess where Miss Jessel is.

SUMMARY: CHAPTER XX
Flora glares at the governess, and Mrs. Grose cries out. The governess grasps Mrs. Grose's arm and points out Miss Jessel on the opposite bank, delighted at having "brought on a proof." The governess is surprised by Flora's reaction, for she looks not in the direction of Miss Jessel but at the governess, glaring accusingly. Mrs. Grose protests, asking what the governess sees. Astonished, the governess points out Miss Jessel again, and Mrs. Grose, seeing nothing, pleads with the governess to return to the house.

Flora, who has turned "almost ugly," exclaims she has never seen anything and demands that Mrs. Grose take her away from the governess. Convinced that Miss Jessel is speaking through Flora, the governess declares Flora "lost" and tells Mrs. Grose to go. The governess gives in to long moments of grief before returning home, noting that the boat is in its usual position. At the house, she finds Flora her usual self and is joined by Miles in silence.

SUMMARY: CHAPTER XXI
Mrs. Grose wakes the governess with news that Flora is sick and terrified of the governess. According to Mrs. Grose, Flora has said nothing about Miss Jessel. The governess, surmising that Flora wants to get rid of her, constructs a plan calling for Mrs. Grose to take Flora straight to her uncle and for the governess to stay at Bly with Miles. She demands that Flora and Miles have no contact prior to Flora's departure.

Mrs. Grose expresses skepticism but decides Flora must leave the place immediately. She states that Flora has been saying "really shocking" things about the governess, who laughs, saying she knows where Flora picked up such language. Mrs. Grose tells the governess she believes what the governess has been saying. Remembering her letter, the governess says it will arrive before Mrs. Grose does, but Mrs. Grose informs her that the letter was not sent—Miles took it. Mrs. Grose then declares that Miles must have been expelled for stealing letters. The governess reveals that the letter contained only a demand for an interview.

ANALYSIS

The scene in which the governess confronts Flora at the lake is a climactic moment, because it brings the conflict between Flora and the governess out into the open, with the governess's explicit accusation. Up to this time, the governess has skirted the issue, with neither the children nor the governess mentioning the names Quint or Jessel to each other. Once the governess makes her suspicions explicit, she passes the point of no return. The governess fails to elicit the confession she is hoping for, instead incurring Flora's permanent enmity and rejection. Remarkably, despite this confrontation, we still don't really know whether Flora and Miles are in league with the ghosts. Flora's reaction could be seen as a vivid and terrifying manifestation of Miss Jessel's control over her, but it could also plausibly be read as Flora's final rejection of an insane governess who has tyrannized and terrorized her with vague hints and questions. If the governess's credibility was at a high point after describing Quint in Chapter V, this episode is the high point for doubting the governess, since neither Mrs. Grose nor Flora corroborate the governess's vision of Miss Jessel.

In Chapter XXI, Mrs. Grose reports that Flora has been making accusations against the governess that are truly shocking and horrible, so much so that she wonders where Flora could have heard about such things or picked up such shocking language—though she then changes her mind and admits she has heard similar things before, presumably regarding Quint and Jessel. As with the mystery of Miles's expulsion, once again we are presented with a mystery, something horrible that is only hinted at. As with Miles's expulsion, Flora's comments to Mrs. Grose could be as trivial as obscenities, or they could be as serious as accusations of sexual abuse. As with so many elements of this story, we are left to imagine just how bad things really are. If we see sexual overtones and double meanings, we can't be entirely sure whether we are projecting them onto the story or whether they are really there.

However, a number of facts support the reading that Flora's accusations involve more than merely bad language. Miss Jessel is a fallen woman, someone who lost her reputation by having an affair, but unlike Quint, she is not a servant—she is a lady. Thus, it seems unlikely that the nature of her bad influence on Flora would consist of vulgarity. Another factor is Mrs. Grose's level of shock as she tries to describe what Flora has been saying—Mrs. Grose actually casts herself down on a sofa as she is talking.

The governess interprets the shocking nature of Flora's aspersions as a vindication, because it seems to prove what a bad influence Miss Jessel was, as the governess has claimed all along. However, another possibility is that Flora's accusations against the governess, whatever they are, are true. In a story where the narrator's reliability is in doubt, any competing view of things coming from the other characters, however cryptic or incomplete, deserves close attention. We have seen that the governess identifies with Miss Jessel despite her horror of her, so it is possible that she has been reenacting Miss Jessel's sexual crimes against the children—crimes that may never really have existed but that might have instead been fantasized by the governess in the first place. This possibility is suggestive but difficult to prove.

Chapters XXII, XXIII, and XXIV

I was so determined to have all my proof that I flashed into ice to challenge him.
(See Quotations, *p. 43)*

Summary: Chapter XXII

With Mrs. Grose and Flora gone, the governess focuses on her impending confrontation with Miles. She senses that the maids and men at Bly are staring at her and reacts by parading around to appear "remarkably firm." Her marching around the house doesn't seem to affect Miles. From a maid, the governess learns that Miles had breakfasted with Flora before Flora's departure. The governess braces herself for a fight "against nature," which will require "only another turn of the screw of ordinary human virtue."

The governess dines with Miles, who asks about his sister's illness. The governess reassures him that Flora will soon get well. He prods further, asking if Flora's aversion to Bly occurred all at once. The conversation continues, with the governess proclaiming that Flora was not too ill to travel. Their meal is brief. When it is done and the waiter gone, Miles exclaims that they are alone.

SUMMARY: CHAPTER XXIII

The governess demurs that they are not totally alone, and Miles agrees that there are "the others." Miles turns to the window. Turning back around, Miles expresses his happiness that Bly agrees with him. The governess asks if he has enjoyed his day of freedom. Miles turns the question on her, asking if she has enjoyed it. He says that, if they stay on at Bly together, she will be more alone than he. The governess says she misses his company—it is the only reason she has stayed on.

Miles's expression turns grave. The two skirt around the issue of what the governess wants to know. She says now is the time and place, and she asks if he wants to go out again. He assents, saying he will tell her everything, but not now. First he needs to see Luke. The governess consents and requests that before he goes, Miles tell her whether he took her letter.

SUMMARY: CHAPTER XXIV

In the middle of this conversation, the governess is suddenly distracted by Peter Quint looking in through the window. She springs up and draws Miles close, his back to the window. Miles confesses that he took the letter. Moaning with joy, the governess embraces him and notes the quickness of his pulse. Miles says he wanted to know what the letter said about him but found it said nothing and burned it. The governess asks if he had stolen letters at school.

Surprised, Miles asks if she had known that he couldn't go back to school. The governess claims to know everything. Denying the charge, Miles says he "said things" to boys he liked. The governess presses the issue. Miles shifts, and she springs forward upon him, pressing him against her. Miles asks if "she" is here. The governess says the "coward horror" is here. Miles searches in the direction of the governess's gaze and names Peter Quint, crying out "[Y]ou devil!" and asking where. The governess yells at the ghost and points him out. Miles's heart stops.

ANALYSIS

On the surface, the conclusion of *The Turn of the Screw* seems to resolve the question of the governess's reliability in her favor. When Miles blurts out "Peter Quint, you devil!" he seems to acknowledge his awareness of the ghost, and he also seems anxious, or perhaps terrified, to see Quint himself. When Miles dies, there seems to be little explanation for this occurrence other than the governess's—he has been dispossessed, and this has killed him. However, if we reread the concluding chapters skeptically, as James has taught us to do, this certainty may melt away. Miles's outburst proves only that he knows that the governess *thinks* she sees Quint and that she thinks Miles sees him too. His words don't really prove that he has ever seen Quint himself. Readers who view the governess as mad tend to speculate that perhaps the governess killed him by hugging him too hard and smothering him. This theory resonates with what the governess has told us about her tendency to hug the children too much and with our impression that her affection is "suffocating," but apart from that, the idea that she literally smothers him is something of a stretch. Miles's death is the last unsolvable enigma of the story.

The governess's final interview with Miles also tells us a little more about the mystery of Miles's expulsion. Miles says now that all he did was to say things to a few people whom he liked and that they repeated these things to people *they* liked. He also admits that the things he said were probably bad enough to warrant expulsion. If Miles's words are to be believed, the range of possibilities to explain his expulsion narrows considerably. He didn't lie, cheat, or steal, and he wasn't violent, abusive, or defiant of authority. His crime didn't directly involve either authorities or enemies, so it doesn't seem to be anything malicious. Among his friends, he talked about something that absolutely should not be talked about, at least not by a boy Miles's age. The things Miles said to the boys he liked may well have concerned homosexuality or something else of a sexual nature. Because *The Turn of the Screw* scrupulously observes the taboo against mentioning sex or homosexuality explicitly, the story insists that *we* supply the answer and take responsibility for seeing lurid and prurient meanings ourselves.

> *Peter Quint—you devil!*
>
> *(See* QUOTATIONS, *p. 43)*

IMPORTANT QUOTATIONS EXPLAINED

1. No; it was a big, ugly, antique, but convenient house, embodying a few features of a building still older, half replaced and half utilized, in which I had the fancy of our being almost as lost as a handful of passengers in a great drifting ship. Well, I was, strangely, at the helm!

This quotation closes Chapter I, in which the governess first arrives at and describes Bly, and introduces the ship imagery that pervades the novella. After spending a day at Bly, the governess finds that her optimism has replaced her trepidation about her situation. Her day has been lovely, largely thanks to Flora, an extraordinarily beautiful and well-behaved child. After one day, however, the governess imagines Bly to be a "great drifting ship" lost at sea. This image appears several more times as the novella progresses and ultimately foreshadows doom. Of course, the gloomy, doom-filled images of Bly might simply be part of the governess's distorted perceptions. We know that the governess is "in love" and possibly irrational, and her eager portrayal of her situation as "lost" seems strange and suspect.

If the governess is eager to be on this "great drifting ship," she is even more eager to be at the helm. Her declaration of this desire is resoundingly cheery, a note of optimism ringing through the impending doom. She imagines herself the captain and navigator of the situation and her passengers "lost." As the novella goes on, she remarks that she is close to port or has just narrowly avoided a wreck. In her imagination, she is steering events. The quotation sets up the governess as a woman eager to think herself heroic. Her attraction to her employer may drive the governess's zeal. In seeing herself at the helm, steering Bly to safety, she sees herself impressing her employer and winning him over.

2.   I was so determined to have all my proof that I flashed into
        ice to challenge him.
            "Whom do you mean by 'he'?"
            "Peter Quint—you devil!"

This quotation appears in Chapter XXIV as the governess points
out her vision of Quint to Miles and gives the narrative one final,
infuriating layer of ambiguity. The governess is determined to
wrench a confession from Miles, convinced that doing so will rid
him of the demon Quint, and she turns to terrifying "ice" to get it
out of him. Whether she succeeds is never clear, and Miles's response
remains open to interpretation. If Miles is referring to Peter Quint as
the devil, then Miles's subsequent death may imply that he is being
dispossessed by the evil demon. If Miles is referring to the governess
as the devil, then his subsequent death may be a result of the governess's terrifying insanity. Miles seems to be indicating the novella's
true villain—but exactly whom he points out is ambiguous.

    The governess's determination to challenge Miles turns her into a
frightening, aggressive woman. Her aggression may be justified,
since she may have a possessed, cunning little boy on her hands. If
this is the case, her methods can be deemed heroic and in a certain
sense successful, since although Miles dies, he is rid of his demon.
However, if the governess accuses Miles because of her own irrational logic, her challenging him is all the more frightening because he
cannot make an acceptable defense. Reason cannot fend off insanity. The governess's description of herself as determined, frigid, and
cold suggests she realizes in retrospect that she may have misjudged
the situation, but again, the situation is unclear. Two paragraphs
later, the story abruptly ends.

QUOTATIONS

KEY FACTS

FULL TITLE
The Turn of the Screw

AUTHOR
Henry James

TYPE OF WORK
Novella

GENRE
Gothic novel; satire

LANGUAGE
English

TIME AND PLACE WRITTEN
1898, England

DATE OF FIRST PUBLICATION
1898

PUBLISHER
Collier's Weekly

NARRATOR
The governess narrates virtually the whole tale in retrospect, as she writes it down in a manuscript. The prologue is told by an anonymous narrator who seems educated and of the upper class.

POINT OF VIEW
The governess speaks in the first person, as she puts into writing her account of the strange occurrences she experienced at Bly.

TONE
The governess narrates with an attitude of intimate confidentiality that is biased and possibly unreliable.

TENSE
Past

SETTING (TIME)
1840s

SETTING (PLACE)
Bly, a country home in Essex, England

PROTAGONIST
The governess

MAJOR CONFLICT
The governess struggles to unlock the mysteries of Bly and protect her two pupils against what she believes to be supernatural forces.

RISING ACTION
The governess has a number of encounters with two different ghosts whom she believes seek to corrupt her unnaturally perfect students, who may be communicating with the ghosts behind her back.

CLIMAX
The governess points to the image of Miss Jessel as proof that the specter exists, but Mrs. Grose and Flora claim to see nothing, which implies that the governess is insane.

FALLING ACTION
Flora becomes ill from fear of the governess and departs Bly with Mrs. Grose, leaving the governess alone with Miles to contend with the ghost she believes haunts him.

THEMES
The corruption of the innocent; the destructiveness of heroism; forbidden subjects

MOTIFS
Vision; a ship lost at sea; silence

SYMBOLS
Light; the written word

FORESHADOWING
During her first day at Bly, the governess thinks she hears a child's cry in the distance. The governess imagines herself at the helm of a ship lost at sea. The governess experiences stillness ahead of each supernatural encounter.

KEY FACTS

Study Questions and Essay Topics

Study Questions

1. *Is the governess the heroine or the villain of* The Turn of the Screw?

We can interpret the governess and narrator of *The Turn of the Screw* as both heroine and villain of the tale. If we take the ghosts to be real and the governess sane, then the governess seems to be a successful heroine who protects her charges at all costs and rids Miles of his demon, thus ending the demon's evil work. If we take the ghosts to be imaginary and the governess increasingly insane, then the governess seems to be the true villain of the story, concocting imaginary ghosts and terrifying one of her students into a fever and the other into death. With deliberate ambiguity, James allows for and encourages both interpretations of the governess. He has constructed a two-sided character who will be of one nature for one group of readers and of another nature for a second group of readers. These two groups of readers are established in the prologue, when Douglas introduces the governess and singles out the anonymous narrator by telling him "you will easily judge" her character. In this way, James alerts his readers that they will have to judge the nature of the governess for themselves.

2. *How does the phrase "the turn of the screw" apply to the governess's tale?*

By titling his work *The Turn of the Screw*, James suggests that the phrase "the turn of the screw" is a fitting representation of the tale. The phrase works as a metaphor that compares a tale's effect on its recipients to a screw boring into a hole. With each turn of the screw, the story's point is driven home, and its recipients are pierced further and on a deeper level. James turns the screw a number of times to amplify his novella's ability to penetrate. He preambles the tale with an intriguing but ambiguous prologue that foreshadows "deli-

46

cious" dread. James turns the screw when Douglas does, with the introduction of a story involving not one but two children falling prey to supernatural events. The screw turns again when we understand that the children of the governess's tale are not merely victims but participants in the realm of ghosts and may even be plotting deceits and evil deeds themselves. With the suggestion that the governess is insane and that she, not her imaginary ghost world, is the villain, the plot thickens even more.

SUGGESTED ESSAY TOPICS

1. *How does James imply that the governess resembles a ghost?*

2. *The governess's letter to her employer is very important to Mrs. Grose and so important to Miles that he steals it. Yet the governess is hesitant to write this letter. Why is this letter so significant?*

3. *Before his heart stops, Miles shouts out, "Peter Quint—you devil!" Who is being named the devil?*

4. *Give two different interpretations of the scene in which the governess and Mrs. Grose find Flora by the lake and argue for one interpretation over the other.*

5. *Give two significant examples of James's use of deliberate ambiguity and offer two different interpretations of each example.*

REVIEW AND RESOURCES

QUIZ

1. What is the governess's relationship to Douglas?

    A. He is her father
    B. She was his sister's governess
    C. She was his wife's sister
    D. He is her husband's brother

2. Whom does the governess see peering into the dining-room window on a Sunday?

    A. Flora
    B. Mrs. Grose
    C. Miss Jessel
    D. Peter Quint

3. Whom does Mrs. Grose see peering into the dining-room window on a Sunday?

    A. Flora
    B. The governess
    C. Miss Jessel
    D. Peter Quint

4. Who claims not to see Miss Jessel at the lake?

    A. Flora and Mrs. Grose
    B. The governess
    C. Miles
    D. Miles and Flora

5. What does Miles do to "distract" the governess while Flora wanders off?

    A. He rattles off mathematical proofs
    B. He plays cards
    C. He plays the piano
    D. He dances with her

6. What does Miles bring up as he is walking to church with the governess?

    A. Ghosts
    B. Learning Italian
    C. His relationship with Peter Quint
    D. School

7. What does Miles confess to stealing?

    A. The governess's letter to her employer
    B. The governess's candle
    C. Flora's hairbrush
    D. The governess's manuscript

8. Whom does the governess see out on the lawn one night?

    A. Peter Quint
    B. Miles
    C. Flora
    D. Miss Jessel

9. Where do Mrs. Grose and the governess find Flora?

    A. On the opposite shore of the lake
    B. Out on the lawn
    C. In the governess's bedroom
    D. In the kitchen

10. What is a key factor in the governess's agreement to take the position at Bly?

    A. Her employer's good looks
    B. She needs money
    C. Her father has died, and she has nowhere else to go
    D. She was a friend of Miss Jessel

11. Whom does the governess see sitting at the bottom of the stairs?

    A. Peter Quint
    B. Miles
    C. Miss Jessel
    D. Flora

12. At whom does the governess scream in the schoolroom?

   A. Peter Quint
   B. Miles
   C. Miss Jessel
   D. Flora

13. What does Quint vanish into on the staircase?

   A. A dimming of the lights
   B. Silence
   C. The wall
   D. The floor

14. Whom does Miles first name when the governess points out a vision in the last scene?

   A. Peter Quint
   B. Miles
   C. Miss Jessel
   D. Flora

15. Who narrates the prologue?

   A. Douglas
   B. Griffin
   C. The governess
   D. An anonymous narrator

16. Where is Bly?

   A. Essex
   B. London
   C. Suffolk
   D. Massachusetts

17. What does the headmaster's letter say?

   A. The school cannot keep Miles
   B. Miles has been bad
   C. Miles is too young to go to school here
   D. Miles has won an award

18. According to Miles, why can't he return to school?

    A. He harmed other boys
    B. He said things
    C. He initiated inappropriate relationships
    D. He wrote profanities on the bathroom walls

19. Where does the governess find Flora when she realizes Flora is out of bed?

    A. Out on the lawn
    B. With Miss Jessel
    C. Under the window blind
    D. In Miles's room

20. Why does Flora leave Bly?

    A. She is going to school
    B. She is going to a friend's house
    C. She wants to travel the country
    D. She is sick

SUGGESTIONS FOR FURTHER READING

BEIDLER, PETER G. *Ghosts, Demons, and Henry James:* THE TURN OF THE SCREW *and the Turn of the Century.* Columbia: University of Missouri Press, 1989.

————. *Frames in James: The Tragic Muse,* THE TURN OF THE SCREW, *What Maisie Knew, and The Ambassadors.* British Columbia, Canada: University of Victoria, 1993.

CRANFILL, THOMAS MABRY, and ROBERT LANIER CLARK, JR. *An Anatomy of* THE TURN OF THE SCREW. Austin: University of Texas Press, 1965.

EDEL, LEON. *The Life of Henry James.* New York: Penguin Books, 1963.

HELLER, TERRY. THE TURN OF THE SCREW: *Bewildered Vision.* Boston: Twayne Publishers, 1989.

LUSTIG, T. J. *Henry James and the Ghostly.* Cambridge, England: Cambridge University Press, 1994.

NOVICK, SHELDON M. *Henry James: The Young Master.* New York: Random House, 1996.

SHEPPARD, E. A. *Henry James and* THE TURN OF THE SCREW. Auckland, New Zealand: Auckland University Press, 1974.

REVIEW & RESOURCES

DAISY MILLER

CONTEXT

In the autumn of 1877, Henry James (1843–1916) heard a piece of gossip from a friend in Rome about a young American girl traveling with her wealthy but unsophisticated mother in Europe. The girl had met a handsome Italian of "vague identity" and no particular social standing and attempted to introduce him into the exclusive society of expatriate Americans in Rome. The incident had ended in a snub of some sort, a "small social check . . . of no great gravity," the exact nature of which James promptly forgot. Nevertheless, in the margin of the notebook where he recorded the anecdote, he wrote "Dramatise, dramatise!" He never knew the young lady in question or heard mention of her again, but he proceeded to immortalize the idea of her in *Daisy Miller*.

A native of New York, James had been born into a world of ideas and letters. His father, an amateur philosopher and theologian who had inherited a considerable fortune, socialized with all the leading intellectuals of the day. Henry's older brother, William, would become a key figure in the emerging science of psychology. In 1855, when James was twelve, the family embarked on a three-year tour of Europe that included London, Paris, and Geneva. The experience was to have a profound influence on James's life and writing. In addition to European art and culture, the trip exposed him to the erudition of European society. It also put him in an ideal position to observe the contrasts between New and Old World values, a conflict that was to appear repeatedly in James's fiction as "the international theme."

Daisy Miller was first published in the June and July 1878 issues of the British magazine *Cornhill*. It was an instant success, transforming James into an author of international standing. The novel's popularity almost certainly derived from the portrait at its center, of a naïve, overly self-confident, and rather vulgar American girl attempting to inhabit the rarified atmosphere of European high society.

The post–Civil War industrial boom had given rise to a new class of wealthy Americans for whom "the grand tour," an extended trip through Europe, represented the pinnacle of social and financial success. As a result, Americans were visiting Europe for the first time in record numbers. However, American manners differed greatly from European manners, and the Americans were largely ignorant of the customs of Europeans of comparable social status. Between these two groups lay a third: wealthy American expatriates whose strict observance of the Old World standards of propriety outdid even the Europeans.

Daisy Miller, fresh from the high society of Schenectady, New York, neither knows nor cares about local notions of propriety, and the conflict between her free-spirited foolishness and the society she offends is at the heart of the novel. *Daisy Miller* has been hailed as the first "international novel," but it is also an early treatment of another theme that was to absorb James throughout his career: the phenomenon of the life unlived. In a novel incorporating this theme, the protagonist, owing to some aspect of his or her own character, such as an unconscious fear or a lack of passion or feeling, lets some opportunity for happiness go by and realizes it too late. In *Daisy Miller*, such a protagonist is Winterbourne, who spends the entire novel trying to figure out Daisy. In fact, it has been argued that *Daisy Miller* isn't really so much about Daisy herself as it is about Winterbourne's wholesale failure to understand her.

Plot Overview

At a hotel in the resort town of Vevey, Switzerland, a young American named Winterbourne meets a rich, pretty American girl named Daisy Miller, who is traveling around Europe with her mother and her younger brother, Randolph. Winterbourne, who has lived in Geneva most of his life, is both charmed and mystified by Daisy, who is less proper than the European girls he has encountered. She seems wonderfully spontaneous, if a little crass and "uncultivated." Despite the fact that Mrs. Costello, his aunt, strongly disapproves of the Millers and flatly refuses to be introduced to Daisy, Winterbourne spends time with Daisy at Vevey and even accompanies her, unchaperoned, to Chillon Castle, a famous local tourist attraction.

The following winter, Winterbourne goes to Rome, knowing Daisy will be there, and is distressed to learn from his aunt that she has taken up with a number of well-known fortune hunters and become the talk of the town. She has one suitor in particular, a handsome Italian named Mr. Giovanelli, of uncertain background, whose conduct with Daisy mystifies Winterbourne and scandalizes the American community in Rome. Among those scandalized is Mrs. Walker, who is at the center of Rome's fashionable society.

Both Mrs. Walker and Winterbourne attempt to warn Daisy about the effect her behavior is having on her reputation, but she refuses to listen. As Daisy spends increasingly more time with Mr. Giovanelli, Winterbourne begins to have doubts about her character and how to interpret her behavior. He also becomes uncertain about the nature of Daisy's relationship with Mr. Giovanelli. Sometimes Daisy tells him they are engaged, and other times she tells him they are not.

One night, on his way home from a dinner party, Winterbourne passes the Coliseum and decides to look at it by moonlight, braving the bad night air that is known to cause "Roman fever," which is malaria. He finds Daisy and Mr. Giovanelli there and immediately comes to the conclusion that she is too lacking in self-respect to bother about. Winterbourne is still concerned for Daisy's health, however, and he reproaches Giovanelli and urges him to get her safely home.

A few days later, Daisy becomes gravely ill, and she dies soon after. Before dying, she gives her mother a message to pass on to Winterbourne that indicates that she cared what he thought about her after all. At the time, he does not understand it, but a year later, still thinking about Daisy, he tells his aunt that he made a great mistake and has lived in Europe too long. Nevertheless, he returns to Geneva and his former life.

CHARACTER LIST

Daisy Miller A rich, pretty, American girl traveling through Europe with her mother and younger brother. Daisy wants to be exposed to European high society but refuses to conform to old-world notions of propriety laid down by the expatriate community there. In Rome, she becomes involved with an Italian man named Giovanelli, and she eventually dies from malaria as a result of being outside with him at night. Along with Winterbourne, Daisy is the novel's other possible protagonist.

Winterbourne A young American who has lived most of his life in Geneva. Winterbourne is the novel's central narrative consciousness and possibly the protagonist. He is initially intrigued by Daisy because of her frivolity and independence, but he eventually loses respect for her. After she dies, however, he regrets his harsh judgment and wonders if he made a mistake in dismissing her so quickly.

Randolph Miller Daisy's younger brother. Randolph is a loud, ill-mannered, ungovernable little boy of about nine or ten.

Mrs. Miller Daisy and Randolph's vague, weak, ineffectual mother. Mrs. Miller seems obsessed with her health and is utterly incapable of governing the behavior of her children. She is silly and clueless, but when Daisy falls ill, she proves "a most judicious and efficient nurse."

Mrs. Costello Winterbourne's aunt, a shallow, self-important woman who seems genuinely fond of Winterbourne. Mrs. Costello is the voice of snobbish high society. She also fulfills the role of "confidante," a frequent figure in Henry James's novels.

Eugenio The Millers' supercilious interpreter/guide, often referred to as "the courier." Eugenio has better judgment and a greater sense of propriety than either Daisy or Mrs. Miller and often treats them with thinly veiled contempt.

Mrs. Walker A wealthy, well-connected American widow who lives in Rome, knows Winterbourne from Geneva, and has befriended Daisy. Mrs. Walker shares the values of the rest of the American expatriate community, but she genuinely seems to care what happens to Daisy and tries to save her.

Mr. Giovanelli An Italian of unknown background and origins. Mr. Giovanelli's indiscreet friendship with Daisy is misinterpreted by the American expatriate community and leads, directly or indirectly, to Daisy's ostracism and death.

ANALYSIS OF MAJOR CHARACTERS

DAISY MILLER

Daisy Miller is a wealthy, young, American girl from upstate New York, traveling around Europe with her mother and younger brother. Daisy is a curious mixture of traits. She is spirited, independent, and well meaning, but she is also shallow, ignorant, and provincial—almost laughably so. She offers the opinion that Europe is "perfectly sweet," talks with shameless monotony about the tiresome details of her family's habits and idiosyncrasies, thinks Winterbourne might know an Englishwoman she met on the train because they both live in Europe, and wonders if Winterbourne has heard of a little place called New York. Daisy is also a tiresome flirt. She has no social graces or conversational gifts, such as charm, wit, and a talent for repartee, and she is really interested only in manipulating men and making herself the center of attention.

Throughout *Daisy Miller*, Winterbourne obsesses over the question of whether Daisy is a "nice" girl, and Daisy's behavior never reveals whether she is or isn't. Winterbourne accepts that Daisy is vulgar but wonders whether she is innocent, and we never really find out the truth. Daisy does often seem less than innocent—Winterbourne does, after all, catch her with Mr. Giovanelli late at night at the Coliseum. However, whether such actions are or are not appropriate is more a matter of social convention than any firm moral expectation. In the end, the truth we find out about Daisy is only what Winterbourne *thinks* is true.

WINTERBOURNE

An American who has lived most of his life in Europe, Winterbourne is the type of Europeanized expatriate that Mrs. Costello and Mrs. Walker also represent. He is also closely associated with New England Puritanism: he makes his home in Geneva, "the dark old city at the other end of the lake" that James is at pains to identify as the wellspring of Calvinism, not out of necessity but by choice. In many ways, Winterbourne is as central a character as Daisy and may very well be the story's true protagonist. Certainly, he is the novel's central consciousness, the character through whose eyes we see and experience everything.

Early on, we are told that Winterbourne is "addicted to observing and analyzing" feminine beauty. However, he does not appear to be a very deep or discriminating thinker. He spends time with his aunt not because of affection or because he takes pleasure in her company, but because he has been taught that "one must always be attentive to one's aunt." Winterbourne seems to hold in high regard what Mrs. Costello tells him, about the Millers as much as anything else. Out loud he defends Daisy, albeit rather feebly, but the whole novel is, in a sense, the story of Winterbourne's attempts and inability to define Daisy in clear moral terms. Winterbourne is preoccupied with analyzing Daisy's character. He wants to be able to define and categorize her, pin her down to some known class of woman that he understands. Daisy is a novelty to him. Her candor and spontaneity charm him, but he is also mystified by her lack of concern for the social niceties and the rules of propriety that have been laid down by centuries of European civilization and adopted by the American community in Rome. He befriends Daisy and tries to save her but ultimately decides that she is morally beyond redemption.

Themes, Motifs, and Symbols

Themes

Themes are the fundamental and often universal ideas explored in a literary work.

Americans Abroad

Daisy Miller was one of James's earliest treatments of one of the themes for which he became best known: the expatriate or footloose American abroad. Americans abroad was a subject very much of the moment in the years after the Civil War. The postwar boom, the so-called Gilded Age, had given rise to a new class of American businessman, whose stylish families were eager to make "the grand tour" and expose themselves to the art and culture of the Old World. Americans were visiting Europe for the first time in record numbers, and the clash between the two cultures was a novel and widespread phenomenon.

James was of two minds about the American character. By temperament, he was more sympathetic with the European way of life, with its emphasis on culture, education, and the art of conversation. Like most Europeans, he saw his compatriots as boorish, undereducated, and absurdly provincial, unaware of a vast and centuries-old world outside their own new and expanding dominions. However, he was also fascinated by the poignant innocence of the American national character, with its emphasis on earnestness rather than artifice. In later novels, such as *The Portrait of a Lady* and *The American*, James would continue to explore the moral implications of an artlessness that, like Daisy's, cannot defend itself against the worldliness and cynicism of a decadent society based, necessarily, on hypocrisy.

The Sadness and Safety of the Unlived Life

If the American abroad was James's signature theme, that of the unlived life was his almost perpetual subtext. Repeatedly in James's novels and stories, characters focus their attention on an abstraction, an ideal or idea they feel they could figure out or achieve if only they could devote their spirit or intellectual faculties to it with sufficient understanding or patience. Again and again, they realize too late that whatever it was they sought to understand or achieve, whatever they waited for, has passed them by and that they have wasted their whole life—or, like Winterbourne, they never fully arrive at that realization. One way of looking at *Daisy Miller* is to conclude that the whole issue of Daisy's character is beside the point, a red herring that distracts Winterbourne from the business of living. In that case, the heart of the novel would be Winterbourne's character, and the fear or lack of passion that causes him to hide from life behind the ultimately unimportant conundrum of Daisy's innocence, or lack thereof.

MOTIFS

Motifs are recurring structures, contrasts, or literary devices that can help to develop and inform the text's major themes.

GOSSIP

Daisy Miller is a story about gossip couched as a piece of gossip, an anecdote told by a narrator who not only was not involved in the events described but who doesn't really care very much about them. The narrator sees the whole incident with detached amusement, as a pleasant way of diverting his listeners. *Daisy Miller* originated with a piece of gossip James had heard from a friend while visiting Rome, but the story had a nonending—someone got snubbed, that was all. James has been criticized for adding the melodramatic element of Daisy's death. In a sense, though, by underselling the story *as* a piece of inconsequential gossip, James heightens the poignancy of Daisy's fate. The fact that Daisy dies and no one seems to care much makes her death all the more sad.

INNOCENCE

Throughout *Daisy Miller*, Winterbourne is preoccupied with the question of whether Daisy is innocent. The word *innocent* appears repeatedly, always with a different shade of meaning. *Innocent* had three meanings in James's day. First, it could have meant "ignorant" or "uninstructed." Daisy is "innocent" of the art of conversation, for example. It could also have meant "naïve," as it does today. Mrs. Costello uses the word in this sense when she calls Winterbourne "too innocent" in Chapter 2. Finally, when Winterbourne protests, twirling his moustache in a sinister fashion, he invokes the third meaning, "not having done harm or wrong."

This third sense is the one that preoccupies Winterbourne as he tries to come to a decision about Daisy. He initially judges the Millers to be merely "very ignorant" and "very innocent," and he assesses Daisy as a "harmless" flirt. As the novel progresses, he becomes increasingly absorbed in the question of her culpability. He fears she is guilty not of any particular sex act per se but merely of a vulgar mindset, a lack of concern for modesty and decency, which would put her beyond his interest or concern. One could argue that it is the way in which Daisy embodies all the different meanings of "innocence" that is her downfall.

SYMBOLS

> *Symbols are objects, characters, figures, or colors used to represent abstract ideas or concepts.*

DAISY AND RANDOLPH
The most frequently noted symbols in *Daisy Miller* are Daisy herself and her younger brother, Randolph. Daisy is often seen as representing America: she is young, fresh, ingenuous, clueless, naïve, innocent, well meaning, self-centered, untaught, scornful of convention, unaware of social distinctions, utterly lacking in any sense of propriety, and unwilling to adapt to the mores and standards of others. These traits have no fixed moral content, and nearly all of them can be regarded as either virtues or faults. However, Randolph is a different matter. He is a thinly veiled comment on the type of the "ugly American" tourist: boorish, boastful, and stridently nationalistic.

THE COLISEUM
The Coliseum is where Daisy's final encounter with Winterbourne takes place and where she contracts the fever that will kill her. It is a vast arena, famous as a site of gladiatorial games and where centuries of Christian martyrdoms took place. As such, it is a symbol of sacrificed innocence. When Daisy first sees Winterbourne in the moonlight, he overhears her telling Giovanelli that "he looks at us as one of the old lions or tigers may have looked at the Christian martyrs!" In fact, the Coliseum is, in a sense, where Winterbourne throws Daisy to the lions and where he decides she has indeed sac-

rificed her innocence. It is where he decides to wash his hands of her because she is not worth saving or even worrying about.

ROME AND GENEVA

Daisy Miller's setting in the capitals of Italy and Switzerland is significant on a number of levels. Both countries had strong associations with the Romantic poets, whom Winterbourne greatly admires. Mary Shelley's *Frankenstein* takes place largely in Switzerland, and Mary Shelley wrote it during the time that she, Percy Bysshe Shelley, and Lord Byron sojourned at Lake Geneva. Mary Shelley and John Keats are both buried in the Protestant Cemetery, which becomes Daisy's own final resting place. For the purposes of *Daisy Miller*, the two countries represent opposing values embodied by their capital cities, Rome and Geneva. Geneva was the birthplace of Calvinism, the fanatical protestant sect that influenced so much of American culture, New England in particular. Geneva is referred to as "the dark old city at the other end of the lake." It is also Winterbourne's chosen place of residence.

Rome had many associations for cultivated people like Winterbourne and Mrs. Costello. It was a city of contrasts. As a cradle of ancient civilization and the birthplace of the Renaissance, it represented both glory and corruption, a society whose greatness had brought about its own destruction. Rome is a city of ruins, which suggest death and decay. Rome is also a city of sophistication, the Machiavellian mind-set. In a sense, Rome represents the antithesis of everything Daisy stands for—freshness, youth, ingenuousness, candor, innocence, and naïveté.

SUMMARY & ANALYSIS

CHAPTER I

I hardly know whether it was the analogies or the
differences that were uppermost in the mind of a young
American, who, two or three years ago, sat in the garden
of the "Trois Couronnes," looking about him, rather
idly, at some of the graceful objects I have mentioned.
(See QUOTATIONS, *p. 80)*

SUMMARY

In the charming resort town of Vevey, Switzerland, Winterbourne, a young American expatriate visiting his aunt, meets Daisy Miller, a pretty American girl, and her younger brother, Randolph. Winterbourne, who has lived in Geneva most of his life, is both charmed and mystified by Daisy, who seems to him wonderfully spontaneous, if a little unrefined.

Winterbourne has never heard of a well brought-up young lady carrying on in this way. Daisy chats freely about herself and her personal life and boasts about her abundance of "gentlemen friends." He feels he has lived so long in Europe that he has lost any sense of the way Americans express themselves. He wonders if all girls from the state of New York are like this or whether Daisy is a calculating seductress, trying to lure him into an act of impropriety that might obligate him to marry her. However, she seems too unsophisticated to have designs on him. He decides she is simply a harmless American flirt and feels relieved to have hit on a way of categorizing her.

Before long, Daisy announces her desire to visit a local tourist attraction, the famous Chillon Castle, across Lake Geneva, and Winterbourne finds himself in the shocking but rather pleasant position of being expected to take her there, alone and unchaperoned. He is still more shocked when the Millers' courier, Eugenio, arrives to call the young Millers in to lunch. Daisy addresses Eugenio as an equal and informs him of her plan to go to Chillon with Winterbourne.

Eugenio responds in a tone of ironic disapproval that Winterbourne finds impertinent. He also gives Winterbourne a knowing look that seems to imply that Daisy is in the habit of picking up strange men. As a guarantee of his honorable intentions and general respectability, though more for the benefit of the courier than for Daisy, who seems to have no idea what is going on, Winterbourne promises to introduce Daisy to his aunt.

ANALYSIS

The narrator of *Daisy Miller* presents the events as "true"—that is, the narrator tells us the events took place "three or four years ago" to a young man, Winterbourne, with whom the narrator does not claim to be intimately associated but about whom there are many stories. The device of the distant, first-person narrator who knows but is not knowledgeable, who is interested but not involved, has the effect of setting the whole story up within the framework of a piece of gossip. This strategy is ironic, since the story itself is about gossip: the things one hears about people, the assumptions one makes about them based on the things one hears, and the difficulty of judging character based on the stories one hears.

As often happens in the work of Henry James, a number of the novel's primary themes are established in the opening paragraph, which offers contrasts between old and young, history and novelty, movement and stillness, and American vibrancy and European dignity. The narrator tells us that the selection of hotels that line the lakefront include many different kinds of establishments, from the "grand" hotels "of the newest fashion" to the older boardinghouse-style pensions. The narrator tells us that the Trois Couronnes, the particular hotel in whose garden Winterbourne is sitting, is one of the "classical" variety, distinguished from its "upstart neighbors" by an air of "maturity." Vevey is filled with American tourists, "stylish young girls" who flit to and fro bringing with them "a rustle of muslin flounces, a rattle of dance music" in the stillness of morning. Set against these vivid images are the European elements, the quiet German waiters who have the bearing and gravity of state officials; the sedate Russian princesses; and the well-behaved little Polish boys whose "governors," nannies and tutors, accompany them wherever they go. These observations set the stage for the conflicts Daisy and Winterbourne will encounter between American and European values and social expectations.

James had a particular gift for capturing the voice and spirit of childhood, and our first glimpse of young Randolph Miller, as he strolls up the path, poking his alpenstock into everything he sees, including benches, flowerbeds, and the skirts of passing ladies, is wonderfully realistic. Winterbourne's first introduction to the Millers comes by way of Randolph, who accosts Winterbourne in the garden. Randolph is a significantly American breed of child. Unlike the little Polish boys the narrator has described, Randolph is allowed to roam wild. He has no compunction about approaching a complete stranger and starting a conversation. Clearly, he has never encountered the European view that children should be seen and not heard. Randolph is loud, ill mannered, overly assertive, and self-important. In fact, he very much resembles a particular type of well-to-do American tourist who boasts of his wealth, thinks everything made in America best, and cannot wait to go home.

If Randolph represents "the ugly American," Daisy may represent the innocent, unworldly America. Like America, she is the beneficiary of a newly created wealth that she displays with more liberality than taste. She is frank, open, uncomplicated, and hopelessly provincial. She thinks the social whirlwind of Schenectady, New York, represents high society and that Europe is "perfectly sweet" but consists entirely of hotels. Daisy has no social graces, such as tact or an ability to pick up signals. She natters on thoughtlessly about whatever is on her mind, happy to regale a complete stranger with details of her family's personal habits and idiosyncrasies. This self-imposition and self-absorption, both amusing and an affront, suggests qualities of America itself that both attract and repel Europeans.

Very little about Daisy is charming, yet Winterbourne is charmed—partly because her inane chatter represents a novelty and partly because she is inordinately pretty and Winterbourne considers himself a connoisseur of feminine beauty. His inability to read and understand Daisy makes him uneasy. Winterbourne is a man who likes being able to classify and categorize people, and he doesn't know how to classify Daisy. He spends the rest of the novel trying to figure out where to place her in the scheme of what he knows and understands.

CHAPTER 2

SUMMARY
Winterbourne has promised to introduce Daisy to his aunt, Mrs. Costello, but Mrs. Costello has noticed the Millers at the hotel and disapproves of them, summing them up as "common." Winterbourne suggests that the Millers are merely "uncultivated."

As proof of his own favorable opinion of Daisy, Winterbourne volunteers that he plans to take Daisy to the Chateau de Chillon. This information only confirms Mrs. Costello's opinion of Daisy as "a dreadful girl." She warns Winterbourne against meddling with girls like Daisy and tells him he has been away from America too long and will make a big mistake if he is not careful. Later that evening, when Winterbourne runs into Daisy again in the hotel garden, she tells him that she has learned all about his aunt from the hotel chambermaid and wants to be introduced to her. Embarrassed, Winterbourne explains that his aunt's health will make an introduction impossible. Daisy doesn't immediately understand the snub. When she does, she merely laughs and remarks, "She doesn't want to know me!" However, Winterbourne thinks her voice trembles a little.

Two days later, Winterbourne takes Daisy to Chillon. He has never done anything remotely like this before, and he is tremendously excited. On the boat over he is a little relieved that she doesn't talk too loudly or laugh too much, as he feared she might. He wonders if she is less "common" than he had initially supposed, or if he is simply getting used to her vulgarity.

At the castle, Daisy is lively and animated, responding with mock horror to all the gothic attractions of the place. History and tradition do not really interest her, however, and she spends most of the outing talking about herself and asking Winterbourne personal questions.

When Winterbourne mentions that he will be returning to Geneva in a day or two, Daisy's mood suddenly changes. She flies into a mock rage, calling him "horrid" and teasing him relentlessly until she has elicited a promise that he will come to see her in Rome the following winter. She is silent on the way home.

ANALYSIS

The reclusive and uncompromising Mrs. Costello represents the snobbish voice of high society, and the fact that Winterbourne takes her opinions to heart casts him in an unflattering light. Mrs. Costello is a shallow, self-important woman whose own children seem to have as little to do with her as possible, though Winterbourne seems quite willing to spend much of his time with her. He takes seriously her assessment of Daisy and her family and defends Daisy only feebly, characterizing her as "completely uncultivated" but "wonderfully pretty." He tries to prove what a "nice" girl he thinks Daisy is by telling Mrs. Costello he plans to take her to the castle at Chillon, but Mrs. Costello finds the fact that Daisy agreed to the trip so soon after meeting him very troubling. She raises the question of whether Daisy is actually as nice as Winterbourne thinks she is. At the heart of Mrs. Costello's suspicion is the extremely European idea that Daisy might be an adventuress—a sort of social hustler whose whole object is to trick Winterbourne into compromising her and therefore obligating him to marry her. Such women actually existed, and indeed, Winterbourne has encountered them in Europe before. However, Winterbourne suspects Daisy of this maneuver almost too easily, which calls his judgment into question.

Mrs. Costello objects to the Millers and mocks their pretensions for two reasons: first, since Mr. Miller made his money rather than inheriting it, the Millers represent "new money," and second, they are vulgar. The Millers *are* vulgar, especially Daisy. She tells Winterbourne about having grilled the hotel chambermaid about his aunt, which is a vulgar thing to do, let alone to admit to Winterbourne. Daisy's speech habits are a clue that James intends us to regard her critically. She talks endlessly and monotonously about herself, with frequent recourse to expressions such as the phrase "ever so" that undereducated Americans thought were "refined." Daisy seems to regard every thought that runs through her mind worth expressing, which is an extraordinary kind of egotism. Daisy is also silly and vapid, and even the atmosphere of the castle at Chillon, with its historic and literary associations, fails to distract Daisy from the business of flirting. Her focus remains trained on the trivial and personal, her own and Winterbourne's "tastes, habits, and intentions." Daisy's almost infantile approach to conversation seems to be a symptom of her larger inability to adapt to her surroundings.

CHAPTER 3

SUMMARY

The following winter, Mrs. Costello writes to Winterbourne asking him to come and visit her in Rome and to bring her a copy of a novel called *Paule Méré*. The Millers are also in Rome, and Mrs. Costello reports that Daisy's behavior has excited much gossip among the Americans there. Daisy socializes with known fortune hunters and appears unchaperoned at parties with an unknown Italian, "a gentleman with a good deal of manner and a wonderful mustache."

His first day in Rome, Winterbourne encounters the Millers at the house of Mrs. Walker, a wealthy, well-connected woman he knows from Geneva. Daisy reproaches Winterbourne for having called on Mrs. Walker before calling on her. She also asks Mrs. Walker's permission to bring one of her gentleman friends, "the beautiful Giovanelli," to a big party Mrs. Walker is giving later that week, despite the fact that no one in Mrs. Walker's circle is acquainted with him. Reluctantly, Mrs. Walker grants her permission.

Daisy announces that she is leaving to meet Mr. Giovanelli at the Pincio Gardens, a favorite spot for strolling and slow carriage rides, for seeing and being seen. Mrs. Walker and Mrs. Miller advise against this, Mrs. Walker because it is not the custom in Rome for young ladies to walk alone in broad daylight with gentlemen, and Mrs. Miller because she fears for Daisy's health. Evening is when people are thought most vulnerable to "Roman fever," or malaria. Daisy refuses to be dissuaded but suggests that Winterbourne accompany her, and he agrees.

When they arrive at the Pincio, Winterbourne is shocked by his first sight of Mr. Giovanelli, who seems to him at best a clever imitation of a gentleman. He can't understand how Daisy can flaunt her relationship with such an undistinguished man, one who appears to be no more than a musician or a third-rate artist, in the busiest section of Rome. Winterbourne finds Daisy "an inscrutable combination of audacity and innocence."

A horse-drawn carriage pulls up. Inside is Mrs. Walker, who has come after them, fearing for Daisy's reputation. She tries to persuade Daisy to get into the carriage and leave with her and Winterbourne. Daisy refuses, telling Mrs. Walker, "If this is improper [. . .] then I am all improper, and you must give me up." Daisy resumes her walk with Giovanelli, leaving Mrs. Walker stunned and hurt.

As Winterbourne descends from Mrs. Walker's carriage, he catches sight of Daisy and Giovanelli, sitting on a bench overlooking the Villa Borghese. While he watches, Giovanelli takes Daisy's parasol from her hands and opens it, leaning it against her shoulder so that it shields them from view.

ANALYSIS

Chapter 3 begins with a literary joke. In a letter to Winterbourne asking him to come and visit her in Rome, Mrs. Costello passes on some gossip about Daisy and, in the same paragraph, asks Winterbourne to bring her a copy of Victor Cherbuliez's *Paule Méré*, a novel that bears a striking resemblance to *Daisy Miller* in several ways. Like James's novel, *Paule Méré* takes its title from the name of its heroine and concerns a spirited, independent-minded young

woman whose unchaperoned excursions with a man excite the cen-
sure of European society and make her an object of scandal. Even
the settings of the two novels are similar: both open at a Swiss hotel
and end in Italy. *Paule Méré* was considered a mildly scandalous
book when it first appeared in Geneva in 1865, so it is ironic that the
proper Mrs. Costello should think it "pretty." James had reviewed
the novel when it first appeared, so there is no question of coinci-
dence in his choice of this particular work. By having Mrs. Costello
request a novel with a plot that so closely mirrors the plot of the
novel in which she herself is a character, James emphasizes a facet of
the cultivated American expatriates' relationship with art: Mrs.
Costello may admire literature, but she does not understand it.

Whereas the first half of *Daisy Miller* is set entirely in Switzerland, the second half takes place in Rome, and here we meet Mr.
Giovanelli (the name means "young man" in Italian), who will
eventually play a role in Daisy's demise. Giovanelli, an impover-
ished Italian of no particular social distinction, is a slap in the face to
the American colonists in Rome. Mrs. Walker, who sees herself as a
gatekeeper to the closed society of expatriate Americans, is stunned
when Daisy asks to be allowed to bring him to the party and
appalled when Daisy goes walking with him alone in the Pincio Gardens—a compromising situation from which she tries to rescue
Daisy. Daisy's free-spiritedness had been only mildly alarming and
annoying in the past, but it takes on a more dangerous dimension
once she takes up with Giovanelli.

We never get a full picture of Giovanelli, mainly because we see
him only through Winterbourne's eyes, and Winterbourne does not
offer the most reliable point of view. We don't really know what he
wants from Daisy, especially since he must be aware that he is help-
ing her to hurt her own reputation. Winterbourne doesn't know
enough to fully denounce Giovanelli, but this lack of information
serves only to make Winterbourne suspicious. One possibility that
never seems to occur to Winterbourne is that Giovanelli acts as a
confidant to Daisy, in much the same way that Mrs. Costello fulfills
that function for Winterbourne. At the Pincio Gardens, where he
first meets Giovanelli, Winterbourne spends a good deal of time trying to figure Giovanelli out. Winterbourne notes that the little Italian
does not behave like a jealous lover, and he seems to overlook any other
possibility for what his relationship with Daisy might entail.

CHAPTER 4, FIRST HALF

SUMMARY

Several nights later, at Mrs. Walker's party, Winterbourne attempts to make Daisy see reason about her behavior. He explains that flirting is "a purely American custom," one that Italians neither understand nor accept in young unmarried women. Although she may be flirting, Giovanelli is not. Daisy readily admits that she is "a fearful, frightful flirt." When Winterbourne suggests that she and Giovanelli might actually be in love with each other, which would be another matter, she blushes and accuses him of saying "disagreeable things." She spends the rest of the evening in another room with Giovanelli.

When the Millers take their leave of Mrs. Walker at the end of the evening, Mrs. Walker turns her back on Daisy. For the first time, Winterbourne sees Daisy genuinely shocked and hurt. He tells Mrs. Walker her gesture was "very cruel," but Mrs. Walker is unrepentant: Daisy will never enter her drawing room again.

Winterbourne continues to call on Daisy, whom he finds always with Giovanelli. Much of Roman society speaks unfavorably of her now. Since Mrs. Walker's party, the American colonists have ceased extending invitations to her.

One day, while strolling through St. Peter's with his aunt, Winterbourne points out Daisy walking with "the inevitable Giovanelli," whom he has learned is actually a gentleman lawyer. Mrs. Costello jokes that perhaps the courier introduced Daisy to Giovanelli and will receive a commission when they wed. Winterbourne says he doubts that Daisy thinks of marrying Giovanelli, to which his aunt replies, "You may be sure she thinks of nothing. She goes on from day to day, from hour to hour as they did in the Golden Age." Mrs. Costello says she can imagine nothing more vulgar.

That day, Winterbourne gets a taste of the indignation that Daisy's behavior excites. A dozen of the American colonists walking through St. Peter's come to confer with Mrs. Costello about Daisy going "too far." Winterbourne pities Daisy and finds it difficult to hear the things being said about her. On another occasion a friend tells him of having come upon Daisy and Giovanelli sequestered in a small room at the Doria Palace, where Velasquez's famous portrait of Pope Innocent X hangs.

Winterbourne visits Mrs. Miller, hoping to make her see reason about Daisy's behavior. Mrs. Miller seems to regard Daisy and Giovanelli as engaged, though she says Daisy denies it. Winterbourne gives up on the idea of trying to place Mrs. Miller on her guard. Meanwhile, he continues to obsess about Daisy's character. He wonders if her defiance comes from the knowledge that she is innocent, or if she actually belongs to the reckless class of women whose reputations don't need to be worried over. He wonders if her lack of regard for convention is a national or a personal trait. Not understanding Daisy or her motivations makes him angry and uneasy.

ANALYSIS

As Daisy's friendship with Giovanelli intensifies, particularly after Mrs. Walker's party, Winterbourne is in the unpleasant position of having to wonder about the exact nature of the relationship between Daisy and Giovanelli. Winterbourne has many theories, but he never confronts the possibility that he himself has feelings for Daisy. He always couches his interest in her relationship with Giovanelli in terms of concern for her reputation. Nevertheless, there seems to be evidence to suggest that Daisy is more interested in Winterbourne than she is in Giovanelli. Besides her praise of Giovanelli's voice and musicianship, she pays no attention to his performance at Mrs. Walker's party. Instead, she sits away from the piano, talking to Winterbourne. She is also strangely offended when Winterbourne suggests that Daisy's flirting with Giovanelli might be acceptable if she and Giovanelli were serious about each other. Even stranger, to Winterbourne, is the swiftness with which she seems to forget her displeasure with him. Daisy's behavior is always inscrutable, but discounting the possibility that she has feelings for Winterbourne is as impossible as labeling her either purely innocent or a tramp.

Throughout Chapter 4, Winterbourne faces tableaux that imply a closeness between Daisy and Giovanelli from which he is or feels physically excluded. His response to these situations is always preeminently moralistic or avuncular. However, Daisy's "improprieties" in Rome are not all that different from the impropriety she committed at Vevey with Winterbourne. She did, after all, go with him to the castle at Chillon unchaperoned, much as she goes around Rome with Giovanelli. In Vevey, Winterbourne was more charmed and titillated by her behavior than scandalized, and once her attentions are focused elsewhere, his harsh judgments may be rooted in his own unconscious jealousy and disappointment that he is no longer the object of Daisy's affections. He may be channeling these uncomfortable feelings into overabundant concern for Daisy's character and reputation.

The scene in which Winterbourne and his aunt encounter Daisy and Giovanelli at St. Peter's clearly shows how the scandal-hungry gossips in Rome operate. Elsewhere, we *hear* about Daisy's effect on the American community, but here we get to see it in action because Winterbourne does. Winterbourne exhibits one of his finest moments here, as he turns from the circle of gossipmongers around his aunt, watches Daisy get into a carriage, and feels pity for her. He pities her not so much because he thinks she is past the point of no return but "because it was painful to hear so much that was pretty and undefended and natural assigned to a vulgar place among the categories of disorder." In other words, he hates to hear Daisy wrongly or too harshly accused.

CHAPTER 4, SECOND HALF

I haven't the least idea what such young ladies expect a man to do. But I really think that you had better not meddle with little American girls that are uncultivated, as you call them. You have lived too long out of the country. You will be sure to make some great mistake.
(See QUOTATIONS, p. 81)

SUMMARY
In early spring, Winterbourne encounters Daisy and Giovanelli at the Palace of the Caesars. When Giovanelli leaves them alone for a moment, Daisy accuses Winterbourne of judging her relationship with Giovanelli. Winterbourne responds that everyone judges her. She asks why he doesn't defend her, and he tells her he does and that he informs people of her mother's belief that she and Giovanelli are engaged. Daisy says that they are engaged, and then, suggesting that Winterbourne doubts her, she says they are not.

One night, on his way home from a dinner party, Winterbourne decides to look at the Coliseum by moonlight and is shocked to discover Daisy there with Giovanelli. The two are standing together at the base of the great cross in the center. Winterbourne decides then and there that Daisy is not the kind of young woman with whom he needs to concern himself. He feels relieved and also angry with himself for having spent so much time trying to figure out how he should think about Daisy.

SUMMARY & ANALYSIS

Still, Winterbourne cannot bring himself to leave the Coliseum without warning Daisy of the danger in which she has placed herself, since the ancient arena is well known as a breeding ground for malaria. He goes forward and asks sharply how long they have been sitting there. "All evening," Daisy says gaily.

Winterbourne suggests they leave immediately and advises Daisy to take some pills that she says Eugenio can give her. When Giovanelli goes for a carriage, Daisy asks whether Winterbourne believed her the other day when she said she was engaged to Giovanelli. Winterbourne says it doesn't matter what he believed. Daisy asks what he believes now, and he says he believes "it makes very little difference" whether she is engaged or not.

Within days, news reaches Winterbourne that Daisy is gravely ill. Mrs. Miller, who proves a tireless and devoted nurse, tells Winterbourne on one of the occasions when he visits that Giovanelli has not come near them since Daisy fell ill. She also passes on a message that Daisy, in one of her lucid moments, asked her to give to Winterbourne. The note states that she was never engaged to Giovanelli and that she wonders if he remembers the time they visited that castle in Switzerland.

A week later, Daisy dies and is buried in the famous Protestant Cemetery in Rome. At her funeral, Giovanelli tells Winterbourne that Daisy was "the most beautiful" and "the most amiable" young lady he ever saw. He adds, "She was also the most innocent." Winterbourne asks why in the world Giovanelli took her to the Coliseum that night. "If she had lived I should have got nothing," Giovanelli says, meaning that Daisy would never have married him.

After the funeral, Winterbourne leaves Rome, but he continues to think of Daisy and her "mystifying manners." The next summer, while visiting his aunt again in Vevey, he tells her that he did Daisy an injustice. He says that before she died she sent him a message, the import of which he didn't understand at the time, though he does now: she cared what he thought of her after all. Mrs. Costello wonders whether Daisy was trying to convey in her message that she would have returned Winterbourne's "affection." Winterbourne reminds his aunt that she had predicted he would make a great mistake. He tells her she was right, adding, "I have lived too long in foreign parts." Nevertheless, he goes back to his former life in Geneva.

ANALYSIS

The scene in the Coliseum, where Winterbourne comes upon Daisy and Giovanelli, reveals Winterbourne at his most pathetic. Nowhere does he respond with less thought or reflection. He immediately takes the fact of Daisy's presence there, at that hour and in that situation, as evidence of her worthlessness. Still, Winterbourne's reaction is complex. He is horrified but also relieved, and he is "angry with himself" for having wasted so much time bothering about "the right way of regarding Miss Daisy Miller." In a way, Winterbourne feels let off the hook, but whether he feared that Daisy was innocent or guilty remains unclear. At Daisy's funeral, Giovanelli tells Winterbourne that Daisy was beautiful and also innocent, which serves as a disturbing revelation for Winterbourne. After all, if anyone should know the extent of Daisy's culpability, it is Giovanelli, her "accomplice" in all her presumed wrongdoing. Giovanelli's comment, which he tosses out as an afterthought, suggests that Winterbourne judged Daisy wrongly, and it strongly affects Winterbourne.

The scene at the Coliseum is rife with thematic and symbolic content. The ancient arena is where generations of Christian martyrs were sent to do hopeless battle with lions and other wild beasts. Daisy is not necessarily a martyr to anything, but in a way she is indeed trying to take on the threatening forces of Roman high society. For Winterbourne, the Coliseum is associated with his beloved poet Byron. Winterbourne thinks of a particular passage in a long verse-drama of Byron's called "Manfred" when he becomes aware of the presence of Daisy and Giovanelli. However, Winterbourne's understanding of Byron is at best superficial, and his thinking of a Romantic poet just here, on the verge of writing Daisy off, is ironic, given what the Romantic poets actually stood for: rebellion and unconventionality.

When Mrs. Costello asks Winterbourne if he thought Daisy might love him back if he indeed loved her, she, for the first time since the outing at Chillon, raises the possibility that Winterbourne might have entertained romantic feelings for Daisy. Not surprisingly, Winterbourne sidesteps the issue, replying only that Daisy meant "she would have appreciated one's esteem." Winterbourne is saying that for all her much-vaunted lack of concern with what people thought of her, Daisy cared what *he* thought. However, Winterbourne uses the impersonal pronoun *one's* not *my* both to distance himself from the whole matter and as if to suggest that Daisy's message expressed something about her relationship with the whole community in Rome. Had Winterbourne embraced the possibility that Daisy's affections and hopes were for him alone, his guilt over judging and dismissing her would necessarily increase.

When Winterbourne tells Mrs. Costello that she was right about his making a mistake with Daisy, he acknowledges her foresight and accepts that his mistake *was* great. In other words, his actions and inactions had meaning for him, and choosing differently might have altered or affected his life. Had he not suspected Daisy of immorality, or had he not denied his feelings for her, he may have found a measure of happiness that is now out of reach. The conclusion of the novel is poignant. James not only suggests that Winterbourne went right back to his former life, but he states this in a way that suggests that the whole story has just been part of an ongoing process of inconsequential gossip, with no importance for anyone—us, the people involved, or the man or woman telling the story. Although Winterbourne is clearly affected by what happened with Daisy, the fact that he can so smoothly return to his normal life suggests that he is, disturbingly, dismissing Daisy and her humanity.

Important Quotations Explained

1. I hardly know whether it was the analogies or the differences that were uppermost in the mind of a young American, who, two or three years ago, sat in the garden of the 'Trois Couronnes,' looking about him, rather idly, at some of the graceful objects I have mentioned.

One of the most notable aspects of *Daisy Miller* is the narrative voice that James chose to recount the story of Winterbourne and Daisy. It is a curiously hybrid voice, neither omniscient nor personally involved. The conventional narrative options open to James were first person, third-person omniscient, and third-person limited perspective, which is in fact the voice in which the vast majority of *Daisy Miller* is told. The voice is third person, and the limited perspective is that of Winterbourne. Before settling into this voice, however, James introduces the third-person narrator by having him speak in the first person—as in this quotation from early in Chapter 1. It is a transitional sentence that takes us from the initial panning shot of the town of Vevey to a close-up of the central character.

   In this quote, the voice of the narrator is breezy and conversational, and like the statement that the scene we are zooming in on occurred "two or three years ago," it has the effect of seeming to place the entire novel within the framework of a particularly delicious piece of gossip. At the end of the novel, after Daisy's death, this voice resurfaces briefly, just long enough to relay the latest piece of gossip about Winterbourne, which turns out merely to reiterate this first report.

2.   I haven't the least idea what such young ladies expect a man
      to do. But I really think that you had better not meddle with
      little American girls that are uncultivated, as you call them.
      You have lived too long out of the country. You will be sure
      to make some great mistake.

Mrs. Costello says these words to Winterbourne when they discuss
Daisy in Chapter 2. The passage is an instance of foreshadowing, as
it looks forward to the novel's closing paragraphs, in which Winterbourne acknowledges to his aunt that he misjudged Daisy and tells
her she was right about him having been "booked to make a mistake." This mistake may be only Winterbourne's error of judgment,
the mistake of having misread Daisy. The context, however, implies
that the mistake is more than this—some sort of error of omission,
something he might actually have done in the context of his relationship with Daisy to change the course of events. After all, Mrs. Costello had warned him against making "a great mistake," and he tells
her that is what happened. Particularly ironic and poignant is the
fact that Winterbourne went back to Geneva, where he is the subject
of the same rumors that there have always been about him. The
implication is that whatever it was he learned has had no effect on
him. His easy return to his former life suggests that the episode with
Daisy may as well have never taken place.

QUOTATIONS

KEY FACTS

FULL TITLE
Daisy Miller: A Study

AUTHOR
Henry James

TYPE OF WORK
Novella

GENRE
Comedy/tragedy of manners

LANGUAGE
English

TIME AND PLACE WRITTEN
Spring of 1877, London

DATE OF FIRST PUBLICATION
Summer 1877

PUBLISHER
The *Cornhill* magazine

NARRATOR
Third-person limited

POINT OF VIEW
Winterbourne's

TONE
Light, easy-going, at times almost conversational; unsentimental; ironic

TENSE
Past

SETTING (TIME)
The 1870s; "three or four years" before the telling of the story

SETTING (PLACE)
Vevey, Switzerland (Chapters 1 and 2); Rome, Italy (Chapters 3 and 4)

PROTAGONIST
Daisy and/or Winterbourne

MAJOR CONFLICT
Daisy's refusal to conform to the strict European laws of propriety that govern behavior, particularly relations between young unmarried people of the opposite sex, raises eyebrows among Rome's high society.

RISING ACTION
Winterbourne meets Daisy and is charmed and intrigued but also mystified by her.

CLIMAX
Winterbourne finds Daisy alone with Giovanelli in the Coliseum and decides she is too unprincipled to continue troubling himself about.

FALLING ACTION
Daisy realizes that she has lost Winterbourne's respect, falls ill, sends a message to him through her mother, and dies.

THEMES
Americans abroad; the sadness and safety of the unlived life

MOTIFS
Gossip; innocence

SYMBOLS
Daisy and Randolph; the Coliseum; Rome and Geneva

FORESHADOWING
Mrs. Costello's attempt to warn Winterbourne against making "a great mistake" about Daisy (Chapter 2) looks forward to his too-late understanding of her at the end of the novel. The scene in which Winterbourne sees Daisy walking above the burial mounds at the Palace of the Caesars (Chapter 4), like the numerous references to "the Roman fever" (Chapters 3 and 4), prefigures her death.

KEY FACTS

Study Questions and Essay Topics

Study Questions

---

1.   What kind of character is Winterbourne? How might James have presented him differently if he had intended him to be a romantic hero?

At first glance, Winterbourne seems the ideal type of romantic hero, but the more we get to know him, the more shallow and unimpressive he seems. This change is largely a function of the way in which he responds to his aunt's views about Daisy. He defends Daisy feebly and takes his aunt's opinion very much to heart. We are told that "he immediately perceived, from her tone, that Daisy Miller's place in the social scale was low." Winterbourne accepts his aunt's judgment as fact. He listens "with interest" to her "disclosures" about the courier, rather than ignoring, dismissing, or hearing them with the same sort of amused tolerance with which he treated Randolph's similarly strong pronouncements about American candy and American men.

James could have made Winterbourne a very different sort of person. If this were to be a love story, for instance, and Winterbourne its romantic hero, James could have shown him to be defiant and unconcerned with his aunt's judgments and prejudices. Or he could have made Winterbourne kind and tolerant of his aunt but essentially independent minded. Instead, in Chapter 2, James begins painting the picture of a man who is weak, albeit in a complicated way. More than anything else, Winterbourne is impressionable— the degree to which he is easily impressed may actually be his salient characteristic. He is equally impressed by Daisy and by his aunt. In short, Winterbourne is a rather shabby protagonist, a young man who is completely a product of his environment and of the values of the society that has produced him.

2.   *How do you think James wants us to view the Millers'*
     relationship with servants?

For Winterbourne's aunt, Mrs. Costello, to dismiss the entire Miller family merely because they allow the courier to sit with them in the garden in the evening may seem ridiculous, and James may even want it to seem ridiculous. Certainly, he wants us to find it funny that Randolph likes to talk to waiters and that the courier should be the only member of the Miller household who can get him to go to bed. However, the Millers' relationship with Eugenio is actually a little sad. Their treating the courier like a friend is probably a function of the democratic American mindset, since Americans did not notice class distinctions the way Europeans did. However, the Millers also speak of Eugenio as a friend—trustingly, almost affectionately. Daisy quotes him incessantly and teases him to his face. This, and not anything more sinister or sexual, is what Mrs. Costello means by "intimacy." Eugenio, for his part, clearly has nothing but contempt for the Millers. He not only finds them vulgar but assumes they are too stupid to pick up on it when he makes his opinion clear to Winterbourne. It is ironic that the Millers' courier should have more sense of propriety than they do, and he seems to be well aware of that fact and to despise them for it.

Daisy's conversation with the chambermaid about Winterbourne's aunt is another matter. This sort of openness is a break with convention on an entirely different level, one that goes beyond matters of upbringing or custom. Grilling a hotel chambermaid on the habits and character of a fellow guest is simply vulgar, and telling Winterbourne that she has done so is even more vulgar.

SUGGESTED ESSAY TOPICS

1.   *Why do you think James chose to call his heroine "Daisy Miller"? Do the names "Winterbourne," "Mrs. Walker," and "Giovanelli" seem significant or perhaps ironic in any way?*

2.   *Discuss the importance of setting in* DAISY MILLER.

3.   *How does health function differently for different characters in the novel? In the case of Daisy's illness, might any symbolism be at work?*

4.   *Daisy makes two trips to architectural sites—the castle at Chillon and the Coliseum. How are they different? What, if anything, do they reveal about her character?*

5.   *Discuss Daisy's relationship with Mr. Giovanelli. How does it differ from her relationship with Winterbourne?*

6.   *Is* DAISY MILLER *more about our discovering what kind of person Daisy is or what kind of person Winterbourne is? Defend your answer.*

7.   *Some of James's contemporaries thought his portrait of Daisy insulting to Americans. Can you suggest why?*

REVIEW AND RESOURCES

QUIZ

1. Through whose eyes do we see most of the events in *Daisy Miller*?

    A. Daisy's
    B. The narrator's
    C. Winterbourne's
    D. Mrs. Costello's

2. How might the hotel Trois Couronnes, where the Millers and Mrs. Costello are staying, be described?

    A. Old and venerable
    B. New and fashionable
    C. A pension
    D. A Day's Inn

3. Mrs. Costello is what relation of Winterbourne's?

    A. Mother
    B. Mistress
    C. Sister
    D. Aunt

4. Why do Winterbourne's friends like to say that he's in Geneva "studying"?

    A. He's doing an advanced degree there
    B. It wouldn't be discreet to say he has a mistress there
    C. They don't want him to sound like a rich, idle slacker
    D. B and C

5. When Randolph first meets Winterbourne, what does he ask him for?

    A. Candy
    B. Sugar
    C. A stock tip
    D. A hug

6. Where does Winterbourne promise to take Daisy in Chapter 1?

    A. Schenectady
    B. Lourdes
    C. Rome
    D. Chillon Castle

7. When Mrs. Costello describes the Millers as "common," she means that they are what?

    A. Like a lot of other Americans she's met
    B. Socially unacceptable
    C. Vulgar
    D. B and C

8. When Winterbourne first meets Daisy, it occurs to him that she may be what?

    A. Less innocent than she seems
    B. A ghost
    C. A transvestite
    D. A handful

9. What excuse does Winterbourne give for being unable to introduce Daisy to his aunt?

    A. She is out of town
    B. She hardly socializes at all
    C. She has these terrible headaches
    D. B and C

10. During their trip to Chillon, why does Daisy get angry at Winterbourne?

    A. He makes fun of her ignorance
    B. He tips the guard to leave them alone
    C. He tells her he's leaving Vevey soon
    D. He recites a long poem by Lord Byron

11. Mrs. Costello's request that Winterbourne bring her the novel *Paule Méré* is what?

    A. Sort of sweet
    B. Highly ironic
    C. Very cool
    D. Extremely annoying

12. What do Mrs. Walker and Mrs. Miller warn Daisy about when she proposes to walk in the Pincio?

    A. The Roman fever
    B. Fortune hunters
    C. Her reputation
    D. A and C

13. What seems to be Mrs. Miller's favorite topic of conversation?

    A. Art
    B. Politics and the Papal State
    C. The "Risorgimento"
    D. Her digestion

14. How does Daisy react when Winterbourne suggests that she and Giovanelli might be in love?

    A. She seems to be angry and offended
    B. She makes the "loser" sign
    C. She burst into tears
    D. She seems to think it's a pretty good joke

REVIEW & RESOURCES

15. Which character, after Daisy, seems least concerned with social convention?

    A.   Giovanelli
    B.   Mrs. Walker
    C.   Mrs. Costello
    D.   Eugenio

16. Which character does not suffer from any physical ailment or malady in the novel?

    A.   Randolph
    B.   Daisy
    C.   Mrs. Walker
    D.   Mrs. Costello

17. At Daisy's funeral, what does Giovanelli tell Winterbourne about Daisy?

    A.   That she was stuck up
    B.   That she was innocent
    C.   That she was ignorant
    D.   That she was wealthy

18. On her deathbed, what does Daisy want Winterbourne to know?

    A.   She always thought he was too formal
    B.   She was never engaged to Giovanelli
    C.   She remembered their trip to Chillon fondly and wondered if he did too
    D.   B and C

19. Many of James's contemporary readers condemned *Daisy Miller* because his representative of American girlhood seemed how?

    A.   Vulgar
    B.   Ignorant
    C.   Immoral
    D.   A, B, and C

REVIEW & RESOURCES

20. When Mrs. Costello pretends to think that Daisy's last name is "Baker" or "Chandler," what is she doing?

    A. Mocking Daisy's family for being nouveau riche
    B. Mocking Daisy's family for having made their money in "trade"
    C. Mocking Daisy's family for not being Irish
    D. A and B

SUGGESTIONS FOR FURTHER READING

BELL, MILLICENT. *Meaning in Henry James*. Cambridge, Massachusetts: Harvard University Press, 1993.

BERLAND, ALWYN. *Culture and Conduct in the Novels of Henry James*. Cambridge, England: Cambridge University Press, 1981.

EDEL, LEON. *Henry James: A Collection of Critical Essays*. Englewood Cliffs, New Jersey: Prentice-Hall, 1963.

———. *Henry James*. Vols. 1–5. Philadelphia: Lippincott, 1953–1972.

GARGANO, JAMES W. *Critical Essays on Henry James: The Early Novels*. Boston: G.K. Hall, 1987.

HOCKS, RICHARD A. *Henry James: A Study of the Short Fiction*. Boston: Twayne Publishers, 1990.

KAPLAN, FRED. *Henry James: The Imagination of Genius: A Biography*. Baltimore, Maryland: Johns Hopkins University Press, 1999.

POLLAK, VIVIAN, ed. *New Essays on* DAISY MILLER *and* THE TURN OF THE SCREW. Cambridge, England: Cambridge University Press, 1993.

TANNER, TONY. *Henry James: The Writer and his Work*. Amherst: University of Massachusetts Press, 1985.